PROBLEMS IN CIVILIZATION

David H. Pinkney,
General Editor

PROBLEMS IN CIVILIZATION

THE
REFORMATION

Change and Stability

Edited with
an Introduction by

Peter J. Klassen

California State University

FORUM PRESS

Published simultaneously in Canada.

Printed in the United States of America.

Library of Congress Catalog Card Number: 79-54030

ISBN: 0-88273-408-3

MARTIN LUTHER. Contemporary engraving by J. Ammann. Reproduced by permission of the Düsseldorf Kunstmuseum Kupferstichkabinett.

ASSERVIT·CHRISTVM·DIVINA·VOSE·LVTHERVS.
CVLTIBVS·OPPRESSAM·RESTITVITQVE·FIDEM.
ILLIVS·ABSENTIS·VVLTV·HÆC·DEPINGIT·IMAGO.
PRÆSENTE·MELIVS·CERNERE·NEMO·POTEST.
MARTINVS · LVTHERVS
M · D · XXXX ·

THOMAS MÜNTZER. Engraving by Christoph van Sichem. Courtesy of the Lutherhalle, Wittenberg.

TOMAS MVNCER PREDIGER ZV ALSTET IN DVRINGEN.

CONTENTS

INTRODUCTION

THE REFORMATION, which so dramatically changed the European world, was born of a variety of causes that embraced the whole spectrum of social, political, economic, and religious forces. To attempt to assign primary significance to any one of these factors is unnecessary and probably impossible, since the sixteenth century was characterized by the interweaving of all the strands that made up the fabric of the age. Church and state were often inseparable; ecclesiastical and political issues were part of a larger complex, and changes in one arena led to changes in the other.

Yet there is also a paradox here. Reformers who called for religious changes sometimes did not recognize just how intertwined various interests were. Thus, when Luther demanded religious reform, many of his enthusiastic followers were convinced that his calls for change embraced all of society. Princes and peasants might well join to condemn various abuses in the church hierarchy; they very quickly parted company when leaders such as Thomas Müntzer also called for a reshaping of the economic and social order. The calamitous end of the Peasants' War demonstrated emphatically that rulers were not prepared to support a challenge to their traditionally dominant position: they insisted on a selective revolution that would single out the church for attack and change but either strengthen or leave unchanged the structure of the politics of power. Luther himself became increasingly conservative as he realized that religious change did not occur in a vacuum and that changes worked out in concert with ruling powers were the most likely to succeed.

The kind of reform desired by the ruling classes is suggested in the statement of grievances presented to the Diet of Worms in 1521. Here, where the newly-elected emperor, Charles V, heard Luther and first met with the German estates, the assembled leaders concentrated their attack on what they described as the "oppressive burdens and abuses" imposed on the Empire by the papacy. The princes and representatives of the towns demanded changes such as curtailment of papal juridical authority, restriction of collection of various dues from parishioners, and reform of abuses among the clergy. The demands, however, did not echo the doctrinal challenges expressed in Luther's writings.

Luther's own assessment of conditions in Germany at this time is reflected in his own account. It is evident that he viewed religious issues as being of paramount concern.

Attempts to explain the success of Luther's revolt have emphasized various aspects of the dramatic history of that age. Some historians have stressed the power of religion in what was surely a religious age. Luther himself was shaped by powerful religious conviction developed through intense inner struggle and turmoil. When he called for religious change, he found an audience deeply affected by a spirit of anticlericalism, ready to follow a strong leader who promised reform of the church.

Other interpreters of the Reformation upheaval have seen economic causes as determinative. Princes and city councils wanted to enhance their economic power at the expense of the church; peasants and townsmen wanted relief from the onerous obligations imposed on them by the clergy. As Friedrich Engels' celebrated *Peasant War in Germany* illustrates, Marxists have stressed the significance of class conflict, viewing the ill-fated Peasants' War as a revolt against the oppressions of the poor. In the twentieth century, and especially since World War II, Marxist historians have devoted much attention to Thomas Müntzer, their hero of the Reformation.

The collapse of the Peasants' War has been seen by many as the end of significant popular impact on the course of the Reformation. For some, the populace became the disillusioned and impotent pawns in the hands of the victorious princes. Yet, as several analysts have shown, the masses cannot be so lightly dismissed. The course of the Reformation should not be identified too closely with the Peasants' War; similarly, the Reformation was much larger than Luther.

Early developments in the Reformation tended to elicit enthusiastic support. Popular sentiment in favor of Luther's initial outburst was a reflection of widespread dissatisfaction and of growing restlessness that awaited the opportune moment. Luther's trumpet blast reverberated throughout the Holy Roman Empire and beyond, often calling forth the support of those who were largely uninformed about the content of Luther's message of revolt but who were ready to follow a vigorous champion of change.

In part, the populace was ready to respond to Luther's challenge because of the widespread malaise of the church. For decades critics of ecclesiastical abuse had disseminated their often vitriolic attacks on the hierarchy of the church and on the monastic system. Calls for reform had often originated from within the ranks of the most stalwart supporters of the church; at other times the attacks on the shortcomings of the clergy were a rather transparent cloak for personal aggrandizement. Princes found it easy to denounce abuses of clerics whose power and wealth they hoped to acquire. Townsmen and peasants were ready to listen to rhetoric designed to convince them that their taxes could be put to better use than to enrich an already wealthy ecclesiastical establishment. At the same time many devout people sincerely hoped for reform simply because they believed the church was in need of spiritual renewal. The church was to be reformed, not divided or destroyed.

With the outbreak of the Reformation an expectant citizenry hoped for change in many aspects of society. Luther's early, often euphoric supporters saw in him a Hercules who would strike down the oppressors of the poor and end injustice wherever it might be found. Insofar as the populace

attacked the ecclesiastical system, political leaders could often make common cause with peasants and laborers. However, when the demands for justice were directed against the social and economic order, the political establishment saw itself threatened and responded according to its self-interest. Indeed, as Max Steinmetz has suggested, an attack on the political leadership often carried with it an implied threat to the ecclesiastical hierarchy. The early Reformation thus soon forced reformers to choose between an all-inclusive revolutionary movement and a selective reform directed specifically against papal authority and certain ecclesiastical practices. Most of the major Reformation leaders quickly asserted their intention of avoiding any attack on political and economic systems; their reform was to be a religious one.

And yet the Reformation was not simply effected by prince and city magistrate. The masses were by no means only impotent or disenchanted bystanders. Since the age was a profoundly religious one, changes in that arena were often regarded as significant victories, even if they were not accompanied by social and economic change. Popular preachers, by gaining support of the populace, often maintained their position by the determination of their followers, regardless of the will of the political rulers. Especially in the German imperial free cities, where the guild system often provided a significant channel for broadly-based participation in local government, religious changes tended to mirror mass sentiment. When such city governments opposed the desired changes, they were usually forced to alter their position, for an aroused citizenry demonstrating in the streets or gathered in the marketplace could be a formidable factor in shaping government policy. The barrage of pamphlets and broadsides, designed to sway popular opinion, suggests that massive efforts were made to influence attitudes and actions. The voice of the masses, though often uncertain and divided, could not simply be disregarded. The fury of enraged peasants, artisans, and town laborers might well be ominous enough to give pause to a territorial ruler and city council.

The role of the populace in shaping the Reformation has long been a matter of dispute. Just what was the role of the people at large in changing the shape of the Western world, in fracturing the unity of Western Christendom? Why did the masses respond to the stimuli of change, and to what extent were they successful? The dominant role of princes and other temporal authority figures has often been asserted; city councils, especially in the imperial free cities, have been depicted as the vehicles of change, yet the manner and extent of decisive popular involvement have remained an issue of controversy.

Reformers often called attention to the need for reform in areas that directly affected the masses, but leaders such as Luther, Zwingli, Calvin, Knox, Henry VIII, and scores of others were not overly impressed with the idea that the voice of the people should provide direction and determine action. When appeals were made directly to the populace, the fear of revolution in the political and social arena soon produced reaction, as the bloodbaths associated with Thomas Müntzer so clearly demonstrated. The spectacle of thousands of peasants on the warpath, destroying lords' castles and wealthy monasteries, and pillaging the countryside, sometimes aided by rebellious town laborers, has too often been regarded as evidence that the popular response did not usually produce lasting change.

Yet, in various forms, the voice of the people did find expression. Lords and councils were often forced to modify their position in order to accomplish many of the goals of the masses, even though the methods used to produce these changes were often controlled by the power structures that had long dominated society. In numerous instances political leaders found that their ability to adjust to popular demand might well determine their tenure in office.

In addition, popular sentiment was often a factor in slowing or stopping the Reformation. Devotion to the traditional faith was frequently so powerful a force, and fear of heresy so strong, that calls for reform brought negative responses. For many, to remain faithful to Rome was more important than to gain greater economic or political freedom. Conversely, many citizens were prepared to allow changes in religion only if political or social changes could be effected. In other contexts, as in the changing role of women, social and religious changes stimulated each other.

The complex interaction of various forces became apparent in struggles such as the struggle for independence in the Netherlands. Here, demands for local self-determination in the face of growing political centralization and religious domination by the king of Spain created a fertile ground for religious agitation. As the struggle spread, proponents of political and economic independence tried desperately to keep religious issues in the background. Zealous spiritual reformers, however, were determined to seek religious reform at all costs. When finally the northern provinces issued their repudiation of the king of Spain and proclaimed their independence, it became apparent that religion, together with economics and politics, had figured prominently in the disruption of the old and the establishment of the new. Such processes were typical of Reformation Europe.

Gradually a new world emerged. New political systems, different religious practices, changing social patterns—all formed part of the legacy of the convulsions that ended the religious unity of Western Europe.

The selections that follow mirror some of the vibrancy of sixteenth-century European society. Many parts of a long-established civilization were shaken to their foundations. Powerful men and vested interests fought for control of minds and social structures. Often men and women saw the issues as crucial, and their actions were correspondingly desperate. Europe could never be the same again.

CHRONOLOGY OF EVENTS

1483	Martin Luther is born in Eisleben
1484	Huldrych Zwingli is born in Wildhaus, Switzerland
1500	Charles, future Emperor Charles V is born
1513	Leo X is elected pope
1517	Luther's Ninety-five Theses are published
1519	Charles V elected emperor
1520	Papal bull, *Exsurge domine,* is published against Luther
1521	Luther is condemned at the Diet of Worms
1524	The Peasants' War begins
1525	The peasants are defeated, and Müntzer is executed
1526	Zurich city council proclaims death penalty for Anabaptists
1527	Rome is sacked by the imperial army
1529	Diet of Speyer warns Lutheran princes, who issue a "Protestation" Marburg Colloquy fails to unite Luther and Zwingli "Reformation Parliament" begins in England
1530	Confession of Augsburg is presented to imperial diet Lutheran leaders form military league
1531	Zwingli dies on the battlefield
1534	Loyola founds the Society of Jesus French "Placards" against the papacy bring swift royal response
1536	Calvin publishes his *Institutes* Erasmus dies and is buried in Basel
1538	Calvin is temporarily expelled from Geneva
1541	Calvin's *Ecclesiastical Ordinances* are promulgated in Geneva
1545	Council of Trent begins

1546	Luther dies in Eisleben Schmalkaldic War begins
1547	Henry VIII and Francis I die Charles defeats the Schmalkaldic League
1548	Charles tries to impose an "interim" on the Empire
1549	Cranmer issues First Book of Common Prayer in England
1555	Peace of Augsburg recognizes religious division of the Empire
1556	Emperor Charles abdicates and is succeeded by his brother Ferdinand
1558	Elizabeth succeeds to English throne
1559	Papal *Index* is established
1562	French religious wars begin
1563	Council of Trent concludes its sessions The Thirty-nine Articles are published in England
1564	Calvin dies
1566	Rebellion of the Netherlands begins
1568	Precedent is set when Transylvanian Diet proclaims religious liberty
1570	Elizabeth is excommunicated by the Pope
1571	Don Juan defeats the Turkish fleet at Lepanto
1572	Dutch "Sea Beggars" capture Brill
1579	The Netherlands is divided into Catholic and Calvinist camps
1581	Declaration of Independence in the Netherlands
1587	Mary Queen of Scots is executed
1588	Spanish Armada is defeated
1598	Edict of Nantes grants religious toleration to Calvinists

CONFLICT OF OPINION

"His Holiness is insatiable. Day after day he invents new devices to enable him to squeeze money out of the German nation.... We also regard it in the highest degree objectionable that His Holiness should permit so many indulgences to be sold in Germany, a practice through which simple-minded folk are misled and cheated of their savings.... Archbishops and bishops have been ordaining base and uneducated persons."

— THE DIET OF WORMS, 1521

"I published the Theses.... The Germans, in the meantime, all tired of suffering the pillagings, traffickings, and endless impostures of Roman rascals, awaited with bated breath the outcome of so great a matter which no one before, neither bishop nor theologian, had dared to touch. In any case, that popular breeze favored me."

— MARTIN LUTHER

"Only Luther penetrated to the heart of the matter;.... 'at once sinner and justified' — this summary of Luther's central idea shows most clearly the contrast between the religious themes which are here brought into mysterious union. The enormous tension and feverish activity which this produced in his religious life is, in essence, the same which in the very beginning of Christianity provided the driving force for a world historical development on an incomparable scale."

— GERHARD RITTER

"The German bourgeoisie and the antifeudal masses were confronted with the mission not only to tear down the barriers to more advanced economic development in Germany, but to open for all of Europe the epoch of the early bourgeois revolution.... the confrontations between the ruling feudal powers and the increasingly oppressed masses made it possible for Luther to develop his ideas publicly and to gain for his part a 'half legitimate' *raison d'être.*"

— MAX STEINMETZ

"The Reformation maintained itself wherever the lay power (prince or magistrates) favored it; it could not survive where the authorities decided to suppress it."

— G. R. ELTON

"The Reformation always was a bundle of factors, political, social, and economic as well as religious. There were instances when factors other than religion were more prominent, even though the official pretense was piously religious. But in other instances authentic religious factors determined and oriented the events."

— HANS J. HILLERBRAND

"Protestant theology came to be related to efforts at political and social change which had received new impulses in the period 1520-40. The one reacted upon the other even to effecting limitation or new moulds for a Reformer's theological views. The small scale of the city enables us to see plainly the development of those relations."

— BASIL HALL

"Towns and territories did not become Protestant or remain Catholic simply because their princes or town councils told them to do so, nor did the populace respond only to any one specific stimulus. . . . although magisterial authorities were often compelled to carry out the wishes of the populace, the magistracy ordinarily still remained the channel through which citizens implemented their decisions. But the crucial factor in these instances is that the town councils or other authority figures were not the locus of decision-making; they were the instruments of the will of the populace, whether townsmen or peasants."

— PETER J. KLASSEN

"While provincial culture at all levels at the end of the sixteenth century remained predominantly religious, its emphasis had shifted from the ritualized, visual effects of the pre-Reformation period to the printed word."

— IMOGEN LUXTON

"The brief, blunt, and vulgar reformation tract intended for a wide and unlearned if not confused audience became a major tool of those who sought change in the religious loyalties of large numbers of people. . . . The use of pamphlets by dozens of reformers in some ways created a Reformation in print."

— RICHARD G. COLE

"City women revolted against priests and entered new religious relations that brought them together with men or likened them to men but left them unequal. . . . In other ways, the Reformed position was more original. A single sexual standard would now be enforced rather than talked about."

— NATALIE ZEMON DAVIS

"The prince of a country is appointed by God to be the head of his subjects to protect and shield them from all iniquity, trouble, and violence. . . . The prince is created for subjects . . . to govern according to right and reason. . . . If he acts differently and instead of protecting his subjects endeavours to oppress and molest them and to deprive them of their ancient liberty . . . he must be regarded not as a prince but as a tyrant."

— DECLARATION OF INDEPENDENCE OF THE
UNITED NETHERLANDS, 1581

I. THE SETTING OF THE REFORMATION

The Diet of Worms, 1521

GRIEVANCES OF THE GERMAN ESTATES AT WORMS

In 1521, the Diet of the Holy Roman Empire met in Worms as the newly-elected emperor, Charles V, attempted to gain support in stopping the Lutheran heresy. In a conciliatory gesture Charles invited the estates to present a list of grievances they held against the Holy See in Rome. The resulting document reflected the deep-seated antagonism toward Rome and also showed that temporal powers were determined to use the occasion to press for expansion of their power.

HIS ROMAN Imperial Majesty desiring the electors, princes, and General Estates of the Empire to acquaint him with the burdens placed on the German nation by His Holiness the Pope and other ecclesiastics, and to make known to him our counsel and opinions as to how these burdens might be lifted from us, we have in all haste set down the following points, beginning with matters touching His Holiness the Pope.

1. *Secular Cases Are Transferred to Rome for Trial in the First Instance.* Our Most Holy Father the Pope, heeding the clamor of his priests, causes numerous persons to be summoned for trial in Rome in matters of inheritance, mortgage and similar worldly concerns, a practice conducive to the curtailment of the competence of secular authorities. We ask that Your Imperial Majesty undertake to ensure that no person, spiritual or worldly, be summoned to Rome for first trial in any matter, spiritual or worldly, but that he be allowed instead to appear in the first instance before the bishop or archdeacon of his province or, if he is a layman and the matter at issue is secular,

before the prince, government, or ordinary judge with appropriate competence.

2. *Concerning Conservators and Papal Judges.* Ecclesiastical princes and prelates have obtained papal appointment of certain abbots or prelates of their own dioceses as judges with jurisdiction over all their legal affairs. Such judges are called "conservators," and they summon laymen, nobles as well as commoners, to appear before them in order to answer charges in secular matters, notwithstanding the competence of secular courts where the cases in question should be heard. If a man refuses to go before such a conservator, he is excommunicated; many examples of this practice might be given. Thus it happens that secular authorities and secular cases are tried before ecclesiastical courts, which are, needless to say, biased in opinions and judgment. And thus the constitution of the empire is violated, for our laws state categorically that no person is to be deprived of the right to trial before his ordinary judge and court.

3. *Concerning Papal Delegates and Commissioners.* His Holiness the Pope bestows upon ecclesiastical persons who so

From Gerald Strauss, *Manifestations of Discontent in Germany on the Eve of the Reformation* (Indiana University Press, Bloomington, 1971), pp. 52-63. Reprinted by permission of Indiana University Press.

petition him special powers to act as judges delegate or commissioners. Armed with such powers, these clerics undertake to summon before them lay persons of every estate and, in the case of failure to comply, compel them through threats of excommunication. . . .

5. *Concerning Ecclesiastics Who Die in Rome or on the Way to Rome.* His Holiness has decreed that whenever a cleric dies in Rome, or while enroute to Rome, whether or not he was a familiar of the pope, his offices and benefices, large or small, shall fall to the pope. As a consequence of this practice spiritual and worldly patrons and liege lords have been deprived and robbed of their rights.

7. *Rome Often Grants Benefices to Unworthy Persons.* Rome awards German benefices to unqualified, unlearned, and unfit persons such as gunners, falconers, bakers, donkey drivers, stable grooms, and so on, most of whom know not a word of German and never assume the duties connected with their benefices, shifting them instead to worthless vicars who are content with a pittance in pay. Thus the German laity receives neither spiritual care nor worldly counsel from the Church, while a hoard of money flows yearly to Italy with no return to us, least of all gratitude. We think that German benefices should be awarded to native Germans only and that beneficed persons ought to be required to reside in the place to which they are assigned.

8. *There Should Be No Tampering with Ancient Freedoms.* A person who holds a papal privilege entitling him to invest others with benefices or offices should not be deprived of this right, nor should he be subjected to legal pressure to give it up. Papal letters or mandates setting aside these ancient privileges ought to be declared null and void.

9. *Concerning Annates.* In former times emperors granted annates to Rome for a limited term of years only and for no purpose other than to enable the Church to hold back the Turk and support Christendom. In the course of time, however, the payment of annates grew into a regular custom, and, as is generally known, the German nation has been excessively burdened with them. . . .

10. *Annates Are Constantly Increased in Amount.* Not only are annates almost daily raised in amount, but they are also being extended from archbishoprics and bishoprics to abbeys, priories, parishes, and other ecclesiastical prebends. . . . Although the old regulations placed a pallium fee of not more than ten thousand gulden upon the bishoprics of Mainz, Cologne, Salzburg, and others, the pallium cannot now be fetched home for less than twenty thousand to twenty-four thousand gulden.

11. *Concerning New Devices Employed by Rome.* The main reason for the constant rise in the cost of episcopal confirmations and pallium fees is the proliferation of offices in Rome. . . .

13. *Concerning Regulations of the Papal Chancellery.* These regulations are trimmed to the advantage of Roman courtiers. They are frequently altered or reinterpreted so as to bring ecclesiastical benefices, especially German benefices, into Roman hands and to compel us to buy or lease these benefices from Rome, a practice which is against both statutory law and the dictates of justice.

14. *Concerning Reservations, Regressions, Incorporations, Unions, and Concordats.* When it comes to such procedures, His Holiness is insatiable. Day after day he invents new devices to enable him to squeeze money out of the German nation and further to destroy the divine service. . . .

19. *Concerning Papal Dispensation and Absolution.* Popes and bishops reserve to themselves certain sins and offenses from which, they say, only they can absolve us. Whenever such a "case" occurs and a man wishes absolution, he discovers that only money can procure it for him. Nor does Rome give out a dispensation except on payment of gold. A poor man without money will not see his matter despatched. A rich man can, moreover, for a sum, obtain papal letters of indult, which entitle him to priestly absolution for any sin he might

commit in the future, murder, for example, or perjury. All this shows how Roman greed and covetousness cause sins and vices to multiply in the world.

20. *Concerning the Depredations of Papal Courtiers.* The German nation also suffers exceedingly from the greed of papal and curial hangers-on who are bent on occupying ecclesiastical benefices in our land. These courtiers compel honorable old clerics, long established and blameless in their offices, to go to Rome, where they are subjected to humiliating chicaneries. . . .

21. *Under the Pretext of Papal Familiarity, Many Benefices Are Acquired.* Excellent remunerative benefices come into the hands of motley persons who claim to be officials or familiars of the pope. They gain the right to hold prebends or offices *in commendam* or "provisionally," or through "regression," "reservation," "pension," or "incompatibility," which causes benefices in our country to decrease and decline as more and more of them fall into Roman hands.

22. *Concerning Indulgences.* We also regard it in the highest degree objectionable that His Holiness should permit so many indulgences to be sold in Germany, a practice through which simple-minded folk are misled and cheated of their savings. When His Holiness sends nuncios or emissaries to a country, he empowers them to offer indulgences for sale and retain a portion of the income for their traveling expenses and salaries. . . . Bishops and local secular authorities also get their share for helping with the arrangements for the sale. All this money is obtained from poor and simple people who cannot see through the curia's cunning deceptions.

23. *Concerning Mendicants, Relic Hawkers, and Miracle Healers.* These riffraff go back and forth through our land, begging, collecting, offering indulgences, and extracting large sums of money from our people. We think these hawkers ought to be kept out of our country. . . .

32. *How Secular Property Comes into Ecclesiastical Hands.* Seeing that the spiritual estate is under papal instructions never to sell or otherwise transfer the Church's real estate and immobilia to the laity, we think it advisable for His Roman Imperial Majesty to cause a corresponding law to be made for the secular estate, to wit, that no secular person be allowed to make over any part of his real property to any ecclesiastical person or institution, and that this proscription apply to inheritance as well. If such a law is not introduced without delay, it is possible that the secular estate will, in the course of time, be altogether bought out by the Church . . . and the secular estate of the Holy Roman Empire eventually be entirely beholden to the Church. . . .

39. *Sinners Are Given Fines to Pay Rather Than Spiritual Penance to Do.* Although spiritual penance ought to be imposed upon sinners for one reason only, to gain salvation for their souls, ecclesiastical judges tend nowadays to make penalties so formidable that the sinner is obliged to buy his way out of them, through which practice untold amounts of money flow into the Church's treasury. . . .

43. *Excommunication Is Used Indiscriminately, Even in Trivial Matters.* Notwithstanding the original and true purpose of spiritual censure and excommunication, namely, to aid and direct Christian life and faith, this weapon is now flung at us for the most inconsequential debts—some of them amounting to no more than a few pennies— or for non-payment of court or administrative costs after the principal sum has already been returned. With such procedures the very life blood is sucked out of the poor, untutored laity, who are driven to distraction by the fear of the Church's ban. . . .

47. *Concerning Improper Interdicts and Suspensions of Divine Service.* If a priest is injured by a layman, or done to death by him, an interdict is generally laid upon the town or village where the deed occurred, even if it was done in self-defense or in other legally extenuating circumstances. This interdict remains in force until the guilty party, or else the council or commune of the town, declares himself responsible. Moreover, interdicts are imposed for debt and other monetary matters, although the Church's own laws prohibit this; but the Church evades

this prohibition by claiming "insubordination" as the real cause of the interdict. . . .

56. *Too Many Priests Are Ordained, Many of Them Unlearned and Unfit.* Archbishops and bishops have been ordaining base and uneducated persons whose only claim to the priesthood is that they are needy. Such people, either because of their low estate or because of some native inclination to wickedness, lead reckless and dishonorable lives, bringing the whole spiritual estate into disrepute and setting the common folk a bad example. Before making ordination, the bishop is obliged to consult six witnesses on the candidate's fitness for the priestly office; but as things are now, the witnesses have, likely as not, never seen or heard of the candidate. Thus our Christian laws are nothing but pretense and sham to them.

58. *Bishops Ought to Hold Frequent Synods.* All the above shortcomings would doubtless be alleviated if bishops fulfilled their obligation to meet in synods with their prelates and ecclesiastical subjects in order to seek the aid and counsel of all the clergy present, as the law of the Church obliges them to do. . . .

63. *Priests Demand Payment from Parishioners Who Leave the Parish.* If a man or woman marries outside the parish, his or her priest demands a gulden as a leaving fee. The parishioner has no choice but to pay it, for if he refuses, the sacraments are withheld from him. . . .

66. *Certain Clerics Behave Like Laymen and Are Even Seen Brawling in Taverns.* The majority of parish priests and other secular clerics mingle with the common people at inns and taverns. They frequent public dances and walk about the streets in lay garments, brandishing long knives. They engage in quarrels and arguments, which usually lead to blows, whereupon they fall upon poor folk, wound or even kill them, and then excommunicate them unless the innocently injured parties agree to offer money for a settlement with the offending priest.

67. *Clerics Set Bad Examples by Cohabiting with Their Serving Women.* Most parish priests and other clerics have established domestic relations with women of loose morals. They dwell openly with the women and with their children. It is a dishonest, detestable life for priests and a wretched example to set for their parishioners.

69. *Many Clerics Have Turned to Tavern Keeping and Gambling.* Clerics can frequently be seen setting themselves up as inn keepers. On holidays, in places where they have proprietary rights, priests put up tables for dice, bowls, or cards and invite people to play. Then they take the winnings, shamelessly claiming that these belong to them by rights of sovereignty. . . .

70. *Concerning Regular Clergy, Monks and Mendicants.* It is well known that rich monastic orders, such as Benedictines, Cistercians, Premonstratensians, and others, have succeeded in wresting secular properties from lay hands, growing daily more wealthy and powerful. In return for the lay properties thus acquired they offer no other services to His Imperial Majesty or other secular authorities, pay no higher taxes and shoulder no greater burdens than those they had assumed in days gone by when very much poorer. . . . Our welfare as a country requires that the orders be prevented in future from taking any more real property out of lay hands, whether by purchase or by any other means of acquisition. . . .

85. *They Try to Gain Exclusive Jurisdiction over Legal Matters, Which Should Be Heard in Secular Courts.* Much legal business that, according to law, may be settled in either ecclesiastical or secular courts, has in fact been usurped by the clergy. For when a secular judge claims a case, it often happens that a spiritual judge steps forward and threatens the other with excommunication unless he lets go of the case. Thus the clergy take over what they wish. According to our laws, offenses like perjury, adultery, and black magic may be handled by either spiritual or lay courts, depending on who first claimed the case. But the clergy make bold to grasp all such cases, thus undercutting secular authority.

88. *How They Take Over Secular Juris-diction by Falsely Pleading Prescription.* Some experts hesitate to call attention to the Church's practice of acquiring rights by possession, that is, by pleading prescriptive rights to gain legal jurisdiction over lay matters, though His Imperial Majesty's and the empire's highest dignities and jurisdictions are thereby being steadily eroded. But we know it to be according to right and law that no one may prescribe, or claim to have acquired by possession, against the high sovereignty of pope and emperor, no matter how many years he has held on to something or used it without interference.

91. *Money Can Buy Tolerance of Concubinage and Usury.* If a man and a woman cohabit without being married, they may pay an annual fee to the clergy and be left to live in shame and sin. The same is done with usurers. . . . A married person whose spouse has disappeared but might still be living is, without any further search for the missing partner, allowed to take up cohabitation with another. This they call *"toleramus,"*

and it serves to bring contempt upon the holy sacrament of marriage.

95. *Innocent People Who Happen to Live Near an Excommunicated Person Are Themselves Excommunicated.* In some towns and villages ten or twelve neighbors of an excommunicate are placed under the ban along with him, although they have nothing to do with his offense. And this is done for no reason other than the clergy's eagerness to establish its authority and to have it obeyed. Because of this practice, poor and innocent people are forced to buy their way out of the ban, or else to remove their families and belongings from their homes. No distinction is made in these indiscriminate excommunications. No one asks: Is the man poor or not? Did he associate voluntarily with the excommunicated sinner? And even though their own canon law forbids declarations of interdict for debts or other money matters, they impose the ban on whole towns and villages, alleging disobedience as the cause in order to mask their illegal and unjust action. . . .

Martin Luther

THE REFORMER'S ASSESSMENT

Martin Luther (1483-1546) is rightly regarded as the dominant personality of the early Reformation. A reformer of boundless energy, he combined prolific writing, dynamic preaching, and resolute action to change the course of sixteenth century European history. Because of a passionate devotion to his cause Luther subordinated all personal considerations to the triumph of reform. Condemned as a heretic and outlaw, he continued in his position as professor of theology at the University of Wittenberg until his death. The following selection is taken from the preface to the complete edition of Luther's Latin works.

From Martin Luther, "Preface to the Complete Edition of Luther's Latin Works," in Lewis W. Spitz, ed., *Luther's Works,* vol. 34, *Career of the Reformer, IV* (Muhlenberg Press, Philadelphia, 1960), pp. 327-334, 336-338. Reprinted by permission of the Fortress Press, Philadelphia. Translated by Lewis W. Spitz, Sr.

MARTIN LUTHER wishes the sincere reader salvation!

For a long time I strenuously resisted those who wanted my books, or more correctly my confused lucubrations, published. I did not want the labors of the ancients to be buried by my new works and the reader kept from reading them. Then, too, by God's grace a great many systematic books now exist, among which the *Loci communes* of Philip excel, with which a theologian and a bishop can be beautifully and abundantly prepared to be mighty in preaching the doctrine of piety, especially since the Holy Bible itself can now be had in nearly every language. But my books, as it happened, yes, as the lack of order in which the events transpired made it necessary, are accordingly crude and disordered chaos, which is now not easy to arrange even for me.

Persuaded by these reasons, I wished that all my books were buried in perpetual oblivion, so that there might be room for better ones. But the boldness and bothersome perseverance of others daily filled my ears with complaints that it would come to pass, that if I did not permit their publication in my lifetime, men wholly ignorant of the causes and the time of the events would nevertheless most certainly publish them, and so out of one confusion many would arise. Their boldness, I say, prevailed and so I permitted them to be published. At the same time the wish and command of our most illustrious Prince, Elector, etc., John Frederick was added. He commanded, yes, compelled the printers not only to print, but to speed up publication. . . .

When in the year 1517 indulgences were sold (I wanted to say promoted) in these regions for most shameful gain—I was then a preacher, a young doctor of theology, so to speak—and I began to dissuade the people and to urge them not to listen to the clamors of the indulgence hawkers; they had better things to do. I certainly thought that in this case I should have a protector in the pope, on whose trustworthiness I then leaned strongly, for in his decrees he most clearly damned the immoderation of the quaestors, as he called the indulgence preachers.

Soon afterward I wrote two letters, one to Albrecht, the archbishop of Mainz, who got half of the money from the indulgences, the pope the other half—something I did not know at the time—the other to the ordinary (as they call them) Jerome, the bishop of Brandenburg. I begged them to stop the shameless blasphemy of the quaestors. But the poor little brother was despised. Despised, I published the *Theses* and at the same time a German *Sermon on Indulgences,* shortly thereafter also the *Explanations,* in which, to the pope's honor, I developed the idea that indulgences should indeed not be condemned, but that good works of love should be preferred to them.

This was demolishing heaven and consuming the earth with fire. I am accused by the pope, am cited to Rome, and the whole papacy rises up against me alone. All this happened in the year 1518, when Maximilian held the diet at Augsburg. In it, Cardinal Cajetan served as the pope's Lateran legate. The most illustrious Duke Frederick of Saxony, Elector Prince, approached him on my behalf and brought it about that I was not compelled to go to Rome, but that he himself should summon me to examine and compose the matter. Soon the diet adjourned.

The Germans in the meantime, all tired of suffering the pillagings, traffickings, and endless impostures of Roman rascals, awaited with bated breath the outcome of so great a matter, which no one before, neither bishop nor theologian, had dared to touch. In any case that popular breeze favored me, because those practices and "Romanations," with which they had filled and tired the whole earth, were already hateful to all.

So I came to Augsburg, afoot and poor, supplied with food and letters of commendation from Prince Frederick to the senate and to certain good men. I was there three days before I went to the cardinal, though he cited me day by day through a certain orator, for those excellent men forbade and dissuaded me most strenuously, not to go to the cardinal without a safe conduct from the emperor. The orator was rather troublesome to me, urging that if I should only revoke, everything would be all right! But as great as the wrong, so long is the detour to its correction.

Finally, on the third day he came demanding to know why I did not come to the cardinal, who expected me most benignly. I replied that I had to respect the advice of those very fine men to whom I had been commended by Prince Frederick, but it was their advice by no means to go to the cardinal without the emperor's protection or safe conduct. Having obtained this (but they took action on the part of the imperial senate to obtain it), I would come at once. At this point he blew up. "What?" he said, "Do you suppose Prince Frederick will take up arms for your sake?" I said, "This I do not at all desire." "And where will you stay?" I replied, "Under heaven." Then he, "If you had the pope and the cardinals in your power, what would you do?" "I would," said I, "show them all respect and honor." Thereupon he, wagging his finger with an Italian gesture, said, "Hem!" And so he left, nor did he return.

On that day the imperial senate informed the cardinal that the emperor's protection or a safe conduct had been granted me and admonished him that he should not design anything too severe against me. He is said to have replied, "It is well. I shall nevertheless do whatever my duty demands." These things were the start of that tumult. The rest can be learned from the accounts included later. . . .

Maximilian died, in the following year, '19, in February, and according to the law of the empire Duke Frederick was made deputy. Thereupon the storm ceased to rage a bit, and gradually contempt of excommunication or papal thunderbolts arose. For when Eck and Caraccioli brought a bull from Rome condemning Luther and revealed it, the former here, the latter there to Duke Frederick, who was at Cologne at the time together with other princes in order to meet Charles who had been recently elected, Frederick was most indignant. He reproved that papal rascal with great courage and constancy, because in his absence he and Eck had disturbed his and his brother John's

dominion. He jarred them so magnificently that they left him in shame and disgrace. The prince, endowed with incredible insight, caught on to the devices of the Roman Curia and knew how to deal with them in a becoming manner, for he had a keen nose and smelled more and farther than the Romanists could hope or fear.

Hence they refrained from putting him to a test. For he did not dignify with the least respect the Rose, which they call "golden," sent him that same year by Leo X, indeed ridiculed it. So the Romanists were forced to despair of their attempts to deceive so great a prince. The gospel advanced happily under the shadow of that prince and was widely propagated. His authority influenced very many, for since he was a very wise and most keen-sighted prince, he could incur the suspicion only among the hateful that he wanted to nourish and protect heresy and heretics. This did the papacy great harm.

That same year the Leipzig debate was held, to which Eck had challenged us two, Karlstadt and me. But I could not, in spite of all my letters, get a safe conduct from Duke George. Accordingly, I came to Leipzig not as a prospective debater, but as a spectator under the safe conduct granted to Karlstadt. Who stood in my way I do not know, for till then Duke George was not against me. This I know for certain.

Here Eck came to me in my lodging and said he had heard that I refused to debate. I replied, "How can I debate, since I cannot get a safe conduct from Duke George?" "If I cannot debate with you," he said, "neither do I want to with Karlstadt, for I have come here on your account. What if I obtain a safe conduct for you? Would you then debate with me?" "Obtain," said I, "and it shall be." He left and soon a safe conduct was given me too and the opportunity to debate.

Eck did this because he discerned the certain glory that was set before him on account of my proposition in which I denied that the pope is the head of the church by divine right. Here a wide field was open to him and a supreme occasion to flatter in praiseworthy manner the pope and to merit his favor, also to ruin me with hate and envy. He did this vigorously throughout the entire debate. But he neither proved his own position nor refuted mine, so that even Duke George said to Eck and me at the morning meal, "Whether he be pope by human or divine right, yet he is pope." He would in no case have said this had he not been influenced by the arguments, but would have approved of Eck only.

Here, in my case, you may also see how hard it is to struggle out of and emerge from errors which have been confirmed by the example of the whole world and have by long habit become a part of nature, as it were. How true is the proverb, "It is hard to give up the accustomed," and, "Custom is second nature." How truly Augustine says, "If one does not resist custom, it becomes a necessity." I had then already read and taught the sacred Scriptures most diligently privately and publicly for seven years, so that I knew them nearly all by memory. I had also acquired the beginning of the knowledge in Christ and faith in him, i.e., not by works but by faith in Christ are we made righteous and saved. Finally, regarding that of which I speak, I had already defended the proposition publicly that the pope is not the head of the church by divine right. Nevertheless, I did not draw the conclusion, namely, that the pope must be of the devil. For what is not of God must of necessity be of the devil.

So absorbed was I, as I have said, by the example and the title of the holy church as well as by my own habit, that I conceded human right to the pope, which nevertheless, unless it is founded on divine authority, is a diabolical lie. For we obey parents and magistrates not because they themselves command it, but because it is God's will, I Peter 3 [2:13]. For that reason I can bear with a less hateful spirit those who cling too pertinaciously to the papacy, particularly those who have not read the sacred Scriptures, or also the profane, since I, who read the sacred Scriptures most diligently so many years, still clung to it so tenaciously. . . .

Meanwhile, I had already during that year returned to interpret the Psalter anew. I had confidence in the fact that I was more skillful, after I had lectured in the university on St. Paul's epistles to the Romans, to the Galatians, and the one to the Hebrews. I had indeed been captivated with an extraordinary ardor for understanding Paul in the Epistle to the Romans. But up till then it was not the cold blood about the heart, but a single word in Chapter 1 [:17], "In it the righteousness of God is revealed," that had stood in my way. For I hated that word "righteousness of God," which, according to the use and custom of all the teachers, I had been taught to understand philosophically regarding the formal or active righteousness, as they called it, with which God is righteous and punishes the unrighteous sinner.

Though I lived as a monk without reproach, I felt that I was a sinner before God with an extremely disturbed conscience. I could not believe that he was placated by my satisfaction. I did not love, yes, I hated the righteous God who punishes sinners, and secretly, if not blasphemously, certainly murmuring greatly, I was angry with God, and said, "As if, indeed, it is not enough, that miserable sinners, eternally lost through original sin, are crushed by every kind of calamity by the law of the decalogue, without having God add pain to pain by the gospel and also by the gospel threatening us with his righteousness and wrath!" Thus I raged with a fierce and troubled conscience. Nevertheless, I beat importunately upon Paul at that place, most ardently desiring to know what St. Paul wanted.

At last, by the mercy of God, meditating day and night, I gave heed to the context of the words, namely, "In it the righteousness of God is revealed, as it is written, 'He who through faith is righteous shall live.'" There I began to understand that the righteousness of God is that by which the righteous lives by a gift of God, namely by faith. And this is the meaning: the righteousness of God is revealed by the gospel, namely, the passive righteousness with which merciful God justifies us by faith, as it is written, "He who through faith is righteous shall live." Here I felt that I was altogether born again and had entered paradise itself through open gates. There a totally other face of the entire Scripture showed itself to me. Thereupon I ran through the Scriptures from memory. I also found in other terms an analogy, as, the work of God, that is, what God does in us, the power of God, with which he makes us strong, the wisdom of God, with which he makes us wise, the strength of God, the salvation of God, the glory of God.

And I extolled my sweetest word with a love as great as the hatred with which I had before hated the word "righteousness of God." Thus that place in Paul was for me truly the gate to paradise. Later I read Augustine's *The Spirit and the Letter,* where contrary to hope I found that he, too, interpreted God's righteousness in a similar way, as the righteousness with which God clothes us when he justifies us. Although this was heretofore said imperfectly and he did

not explain all things concernin
clearly, it nevertheless was
God's righteousness with whicl
fied was taught. Armed more fully with these thoughts, I began a second time to interpret the Psalter. And the work would have grown into a large commentary, if I had not again been compelled to leave the work begun, because Emperor Charles V in the following year convened the diet at Worms.

I relate these things, good reader, so that, if you are a reader of my puny works, you may keep in mind, that, as I said above, I was all alone and one of those who, as Augustine says of himself, have become proficient by writing and teaching. I was not one of those who from nothing suddenly become the topmost, though they are nothing, neither have labored, nor been tempted, nor become experienced, but have with one look at the Scriptures exhausted their entire spirit.

II. THE SHAPING OF THE REFORMATION

Gerhard Ritter

RELIGIOUS CONVICTION AS A HISTORICAL FORCE

Gerhard Ritter (1888-1967) devoted a lifetime of scholarship to the study of the Reformation. From 1925 until his retirement he served as professor of modern history at the University of Freiburg, and for three decades he edited (later, with an American counterpart) the *Archiv fuer Reformationsgeschichte.* His publications include biographies of Luther, Frederick the Great, Bismarck, and others, as well as numerous articles. After World War II Ritter emerged as one of the most respected critics of the Marxist interpretations of the Reformation. His emphasis upon religious motivations is evident in the following selection.

IT WILL SOON become clear that the central task in any study of the life of Luther is to penetrate to the roots of his personality, into the innermost regions of his spirituality. It may be that biographers of other great spiritual leaders have found it easy to pass from the external to the internal, from the historical environment to the core of the personality as it gradually develops in response to external influences. Luther's spiritual development has its starting point in the depths of his soul, where no external influence could penetrate. Whoever wishes to understand him must seek him first in his solitude. Of course, the fact that, in contrast to so many other medieval movements which were quickly suppressed, Luther's efforts met with such great external success, was due amongst other things to a most remarkable and unique set of external circumstances which also claim their place in history; but the real secret of his power cannot be found here but in the period of his spiritual development, the foundations of which had been laid long before he stepped out into public life. It can only be found in a spiritual life of such force and depth that nothing comparable to it can be found in the Middle Ages, in spite of all the traces it betrays of its origins in that period. How many had already tried in vain to break the spell of the priestly domination of the medieval church! Some had failed because they could not really break away from the idea of the church as a sacramental institution; others because they gave expression, less to their religious experience than to the rationalistic criticisms of secular thought; a third group (among them forerunners like Wycliffe and Hus) because their opposition was at first inflamed by the external abuses of Church life and was thus from the start tainted with earthly and political demands before they penetrated to the fundamental spiritual issues; but the one thing which all these men had been unable to do was achieved by the monk from Wittenberg with his deeply spiritual and religious firmness of will. It was out of the innermost stirrings of this will that were to come the most far-reaching historical consequences, because it had to draw all its strength from a source

From Gerhard Ritter, *Luther, His Life and Work,* trans. by John Riches (Harper and Row, New York, 1963), pp. 23-24, 28-32, 43-45, 47-49. Reprinted by permission of Harper and Row.

which lay beyond the reach of all human and earthly endeavour. The spiritual struggles of this man have become history to an extent which is indeed rare. One is immediately reminded of the great mysterious figures who stand at the very beginning of the history of religion; but they are obscured in the half-light of semilegendary traditions. while the picture of Martin Luther is already bathed in the full light of historical knowledge. . . .

His "conversion" in the monastery is one of the most disputed points in recent research on Luther. Nevertheless nothing has become clearer than that one cannot in any sense speak of a once-and-for-all conversion. What we see before us is a hard, wearisome struggle step by step over more than ten years in which there are indeed moments of joyful elation, occasioned by moments of sudden insight, but in no sense that flash of enlightenment which in a moment buries an old existence in darkness and opens up a new path clearly in front of one's eyes. "His soul was the battleground of two ages." Even this does not express an entirely accurate view. For this monk with his deep anxiety about the merciful nature of God is not consciously seeking a new answer to old problems. One cannot stress this point too firmly. No echo of the universal opposition to the secularised papal church and its assumption of worldly power can be found in the loneliness of the purely personal struggles in which Luther freed himself from the spiritual world of the Middle Ages and fought for the courage to live on the basis of a new and infinitely deeper understanding of the message of salvation.

The form which these struggles assumed is well enough known, at least in its outward pattern: his crippling feeling of sin; his terror of the wrath of God, which he tried in vain to placate by intense contrition, ascetic penances and an ordered sanctification of his way of life. "If ever a monk got to heaven by monkery, I would have got there too; all my brothers will testify to that. For if it had gone on much longer, I would simply have martyred myself to death with vigils, prayers, reading and other work." This was no exaggeration; during his whole life

his body never recovered from the effects of these years. But where did this powerful need for the self-mortification of the earthly man stem from? It is in no sense a purely artificial product of the cloister, just as his fear of sin cannot simply be explained as a "monkish disease." It may indeed be that even before his entry into the monastery Luther had at times felt a burning desire to be reconciled with God through the ascetic life (although in fact we have little specific knowledge of this); and yet he would have been able to find ways and means of having the hurried vow at Stotternheim annulled. What then was the root of all these fears?

People have often tried to produce a psychological or rather medical explanation for his case, and it does suggest itself very readily for a young man of heated temperament. If one reads how Luther portrays the power of original sin, the evil desire which rages like a devouring fire in our veins and destroys all free will, then it is difficult, even if one is without prejudice on the subject, to avoid the impression that it is the sensual passions in a sexual sense which he is describing. But it is unlikely that temptations of this kind played a particularly important part in the life of the young monk. The testimony of all the sources, even when subjected to the most searching inquiry by bitter opponents, speaks against this. It is no mere chance that the vow of celibacy was the last of all the Catholic vows which the reformer renounced. The internal trials which tormented him most of all were set on a much higher plane. They disturbed him as profoundly in old age as in his youth; the only difference was that as he grew older the outward occasion of these trials changed and that above all he had meanwhile achieved an incomparably greater insight into the means of overcoming them. He was never seriously concerned with temptations of a worldly nature, with the struggle of the natural man with the strict monastic vows. All this lies far beneath him, and one can make no more radical misjudgment of him than if one sees his soul as the scene of a battle in which the natural desire for happiness of the earthly man struggled against the ascetic's longing for salvation. It was not that the asceticism of the monastery seemed to him too strict and too impossibly hard to fulfil, but that it seemed totally inadequate in face of the infinite demands of the divine commandment. Nor was it longing for heaven or fear of hell which rent his soul; his own personal well-being fades into total insignificance by comparison with the terrible force with which his spirit was torn by the question of an ethical religion as such.

A more accurate interpretation of his distress of soul may be found not in a "natural" but in a theological explanation, which takes as its starting point the internal tensions of late medieval piety. These sprang from the difficulty of reconciling man's free will in his own actions with the ideas of predestination forged by men like William of Ockham, that is from the internal contradiction between the idea of the retributive justice of God and his irrational and arbitrary election of men. On the one side stood the ability and duty of man in his free will to make himself worthy to receive grace by preparatory works, the ability particularly to produce in himself by means of self-abasement a complete hatred of evil and an infinite love of God; on the other hand the dependence of all moral achievement, of all worth in the eyes of God, on the mysterious cooperation of the grace of God poured into the sacraments, which grace (unaccountably only present in the sacrament through the mediation of a priest) immediately disappears as soon as a mortal sin gains a foothold in a man's heart. Against both these there is God's arbitrary decision either to reject or to accept the works of the man which have been produced in this state of grace; to destine the sinner for eternal salvation or eternal damnation as an act of grace apparently without rhyme or reason. So many propositions, so many doubts and questions, so much cause for inner uncertainty and new fear. In this theology a lively active will meant everything and pious abandonment to God was of no real importance (quite in accordance with the English attitude to the world and life, as one would indeed expect from its ancestry). By

its strong emphasis on the responsibility laid on man in his free will and at the same time on the unfettered arbitrariness of God's decisions, it forced the antinomies which are of necessity always to be found slumbering in any high religiosity, right out into the open. One can imagine the effect this must have had on the monk in Erfurt with his intense German sincerity and penetrating insight, as he attempted with trembling conscience to fulfil the moral demands of such a theology and to unravel its secrets with his restless, searching intellect. How could he approach with composure a God on whose grace he could not count with certainty, when his whole life was one long struggle to make himself worthy of this grace? In such circumstances does not justice come to be more a matter for fear than for hope? Did he not indeed have cause for despair as he contemplated a life full of uncertainty and unending yet fruitless striving for righteousness?

Our understanding of these things and of the religious ideas with which Luther was in daily contact in the monastery has undoubtedly been deepened by the extensive research which has been made into Late Scholastic theology in the last few decades. Even this does not bring us right to the heart of Luther's problem. Countless others had had to deal with the problem of this internal contradiction in their religious ideas. Why then was it that it was only in his case that it led to such violent explosions? Whence comes this new conscience which made him feel this dilemma so deeply and directly—to such an infinitely greater extent than the rest of the world around him and in fact than any other theologian since the days of Augustine? Only now do we arrive at the secret of his greatness: that he was infinitely more than a theologian, that in a strange way for a man in the sixteenth century after 1500 years of Christianity he was able in spite of his scholastic heritage and upbringing to remain ultimately independent of all doctrinal traditions; that he was able to grasp anew the external mysteries of the divine in an utterly original manner. It is only when one passes beyond all rational concepts and the questions of doubt which they raise, that the primary religious phenomenon becomes visible. It cannot be compassed in words, but at least an echo remains here and there struggling for expression. . . .

Again and again men had tried to reform the Church without the necessary means; by imitating the external forms of early Christian community life or by putting indiscriminate emphasis on the literal meaning of isolated early Christian doctrines. Only Luther penetrated to the heart of the matter; his mission was not to re-establish the forms of early Christian life and doctrine, but to reveal the religious strength of the Christian tradition in a way which was closely related to the spirit of the earliest beginnings. In so doing he in fact discovered what was at the same time the oldest heritage in the Christian tradition. It was the all-dominating central idea of God's holiness and majesty, casting aside all men's claims to self-sufficiency, unconditional and unlimited in its moral demands, and yet at the same time God who is the Father who has pity on the fallen son, on the sinful creature in all his inadequacy as much as on the man made pure and raised again to a new dignity by moral effort and sanctification in worship. The inconceivable paradox of Christian teaching, which is intolerable to all those who are sensitive about man's natural dignity, and which pours scorn on all the humanist ideas of morality, was again lived out and preached by Luther with rugged determination: that even the noblest efforts of man as such are vanity before God; that all human virtue, even in its noblest form, is as far from the goal of divine holiness as are the highest mountains of the earth from the infinite distance of the heavens; that all our striving towards God will never bring us to him; that there is no possibility of invoking God's mercy, not even of influencing it, even through the highest moral achievements; but that nevertheless the majesty of the Eternal and Holy One can make a covenant with the transitory and guilt-laden creature, because he comes to us with merciful love. A paradox which is not softened but taken to

the point of mystery by the Pauline "Theology of the Cross," the doctrine of the incarnate God, whose sacrificial death on the cross should, in Luther's mind, act as a revelation and mediation of God's merciful will to us, and not as a trial forced upon us; this incarnate God was the most certain, indeed the only certain, revelation of his fatherly love. Truly a highly paradoxical doctrine, which, as Luther characteristically expresses it, "allows God to have the victory over God." If this, as has been said, shows the true mark of the Christian religion as against all other salvation religions—the unheard-of teaching that God has mercy on the sinner and not on the just man—then Martin Luther did in fact achieve nothing less than the re-establishment of the religious mysteries of Christianity with its strange primitive power, and in doing so he consciously flouted the attempts of scholastic philosophy to make it more accessible to human reason. "At once sinner and justified"—this summary of Luther's central idea shows most clearly the contrast between the religious themes which are here brought into mysterious union; the enormous tension and feverish activity which this produced in his religious life is, in essence, the same which in the very beginnings of Christianity provided the driving force for a world historical development on an incomparable scale. There is something terrifying in the bold way in which Luther dares to speak of these tensions. "No one is nearer to God than those in despair, who (in their trials) hate and curse God, and none of God's sons would be more dear and welcome to him. For they make more recompense for their sins in a single moment than if you did penance on bread and water for many years."

This is the spiritual temper of the man who, tested and strengthened in his spiritual struggle for life and death, would one day step out of his monastery cell on to the stage of the world. . . .

For practically every stage of his rapid rise to academic honours there are fortunate new finds of manuscripts which cast most interesting light on the subject: an abundance of lecture notebooks, memoranda, and jottings of various types, whose study, interpretation and evaluation is still today awaiting completion. They show us Luther as a scholar, as the connoisseur and exponent of a centuries-old literary tradition, as a systematic thinker working out step by step his theological terms from the most penetrating study of the Bible, but with constant reference to the great Church Fathers, and above all to Augustine. He appears in a light which earlier generations who had only known his popular and polemical writings had never suspected. . . .

Nevertheless it is decisive in an understanding of Luther's life-work to know that he never based his right to proclaim a new teaching on a special gift of the spirit, on an extraordinary vocation by any sort of divine suggestion or miraculous revelation, as do most religious leaders of mankind, but exclusively—quite simply and naïvely—on pure study, on his profession (not even of his own choosing) as "Doctor of the Holy Scriptures." He never even thought or intended to say anything really new with his understanding of Christian truth—indeed he would have despaired if he had had to force himself to this judgment of his work. Even the formulations of scholastic theology, in which he interpreted his religious experience for himself and for others, were for him in no way a mere expedient which he accepted for want of any better; they were indispensable to him because they ensured the unbroken continuity of the Christian tradition, of which he saw himself as the reformer and not the destroyer or overthrower. Just as he would never rely on pure meditation, on the intuitions of the "inner light," but only on the firm and clear word of the Bible—in this sense a true son of late medieval biblical theology with admittedly a particularly radical inclination against traditional post-biblical doctrine—similarly his religious experience would never allow him to rest until he had fitted it (sometimes not without ambiguities) into the firm system of the traditional early Christian doctrine of Christ's all-sufficient saving act. This rooting of highly personal experience into a world of ideas which traditionally were held to be universally valid was certainly not without danger. But on the other hand one can see clearly how this very thing, the anchoring of his own corpus of belief in the traditional world of ideas of the Church, enabled him to be the first to achieve that highly original compromise between revolution and restoration, which is the essence of the Reformation: and this in the founding of a new Church, which, in spite of all, set out with the sole aim of reviving and continuing the old.

Max Steinmetz

CLASS CONFLICT AND THE REFORMATION

During the past three decades Karl Marx University in Leipzig has emerged as one of the most significant and productive centers of Marxist interpretation of the Reformation. As professor of history at this school,

From Max Steinmetz, *Deutschland von 1476 bis 1648* (VEB Deutscher Verlag der Wissenschaften, Berlin, 1965), pp. 86, 97-100, 105, 106, 184, 185. Translated by the editor. Reprinted by permission of the VEB Deutscher Verlag der Wissenschaften, Berlin, DDR.

Max Steinmetz has come to be recognized as one of the most respected authorities in the field. In works such as *Deutschland von 1476 bis 1648* (Berlin, 1965), *Der deutsche Bauernkrieg und Thomas Müntzer* (which he edited and to which he contributed an article), (Leipzig, 1976), and numerous other scholarly studies, he has demonstrated that Marxist Reformation scholarship in the German Democratic Republic must be taken seriously.

T HE GERMAN bourgeoisie and the antifeudal masses were confronted with the mission not only to tear down the barriers to more advanced economic development in Germany, but to open for all Europe the epoch of the early bourgeois revolution.

Secular feudalism could not be attacked in any land or in any isolated setting until its "central sacred organization," the "great international center of the feudal system," the Roman Catholic Church, had been demolished. Since the objective and the subjective conditions for this first fully developed in Germany, the German people first had this task in Europe.

Germany became the scene of these confrontations because in 1500 it was seized by a deep crisis which held ruler and ruled in its grip; because it was the chief object of exploitation of the papal church; and because at almost all levels of society there was an uncompromising hatred of the plundering by Rome. The ideology which became the banner of the anti-Roman struggle was clothed in religion, and so widely held that it could attract all levels of society and not exclude any progressive, struggling elements. Finally, the confrontations between the ruling feudal powers and the increasingly oppressed masses made it possible for Luther to develop his ideas publicly and to gain for his party a "half legitimate" *raison d'être*.

The national struggle against Rome did not mean that the crisis which had gripped Germany had been overcome; it did, however, show the way to a solution. The Reformation which began with the posting of Luther's Theses was the signal for a general attack on the feudal system, the beginning of the early bourgeois revolution in Europe.

After 1519 the Lutheran aspirations grew into a genuinely national movement which included or touched all classes and levels of the German people, and found a powerful response. The rapidity with which the progressive ideas spread demonstrates the extent to which the various territories of Germany had grown together. Luther's writings were republished in large editions in many places, and found their way into Spain, Italy and France. The number of students at the University of Wittenberg grew rapidly, and threatened to exceed those at Leipzig. The monks, who at first had dismissed the Lutheran indulgence struggle as a "monks' quarrel," became increasingly interested in the Wittenberg professor. . . .

Three walls were to be broken down: the teaching of the two peoples, two powers, two laws. With unprecedented clarity, Luther designated the religious office as a "calling" of the laity, which should choose its church servants from within its own midst. He denied the traditional distinction between the worth of clergy and laity, a position which he later was forced increasingly to modify because of his close ties to the princely powers. The free election of the pastor was included as one of the most important demands in the programs of the peasants' revolt.

First of all, Luther simply demanded the secularization of the property of the church, the dissolution of the orders, and the secularization of the ecclesiastical principalities. Cloisters were to be transformed into public schools or hospitals. Expropriation of the old church was no longer to be regarded as robbery of God, but rather as a God-pleasing act. Thus, Luther also sanctioned earlier attacks on the secular possessions of the church. More importantly, he discarded deeply rooted traditional inhibitions which still blocked a general attack on the material might of the church; he allowed a small brook of "quiet" secularization to swell into a rushing torrent. . . .

The unexpected intensification of the class conflict in Germany from 1517 to 1521, especially the antagonism between the two main classes, led to a situation in which every attack on the papacy and the spiritual feudality necessarily eventually merged with attacks on temporal princes and the whole feudal system. Only the result of this attack on the entire feudal system could determine whether or not the Roman influence would finally be ended in Germany. . . .

Luther's decision in this situation was determined not only by his personal development, but much more by those decisive social forces which he came increasingly to represent. . . .

The Reformation in the cities, often carried out in the face of opposition from the councils, showed the bourgeoisie and masses in action. On the land the estates offered support, and throughout the lower Rhenish area the seats of the nobility became refuges and gathering places for the preachers. One must, however, remember that here and in the various parts of the

county of Nassau the political influence of the landgraviate of Hesse strengthened the backbone of the Reformation forces.

In northeastern Germany the Reformation experienced its greatest territorial expansion, but it was usually imposed "from above." From 1532 to 1534 the new order was established in the principality of Anhalt, in 1533 in the County of Schwarzburg; in 1534 the Pomeranian dukes followed the Saxon model and adopted the new teaching. In the same year parts of Mecklenburg became Protestant.

Similarly, in the upper German cities . . . the modified Lutheran teachings triumphed. . . . In about 1540 three powerful territorial states left the old church. Under Elector Frederick II (1544-1556) the Reformation of the Palatinate, including the Upper Palatinate, began. Following the death of Duke George of Saxony in 1539, his Protestant brother and successor, Heinrich (1539-1541), tried to introduce the new teaching. At first the nobility of Meissen and the patrician councils of the larger cities virtually stopped the prince. The estates succeeded in gaining control over the cloisters and ecclesiastical foundations. Then, with the accession of Moritz (1541-1553), the Reformation was resolutely established. In 1540 Elector Joachim II of Brandenburg chose the Reformation, but at the same time tried to find a middle way between Wittenberg and Rome.

G. R. Elton

POLITICAL LEADERS
AS DETERMINATIVE FACTORS IN THE REFORMATION

Students of history have long recognized the *New Cambridge Modern History* as one of the great works of historical reference. The second

From G. R. Elton, ed., *The New Cambridge Modern History*, II, *The Reformation* (Cambridge University Press, Cambridge, 1958), p. 5. Reprinted by permission of the Cambridge University Press.

volume in the series, *The Reformation, 1520-1559*, was edited by G. R. Elton, professor of history at Cambridge University. His numerous published works include *Renaissance and Reformation: 1300-1648* (New York, 1963); *England Under the Tudors* (London, 1954); and *Reformation Europe, 1517-1555* (New York, 1966).

T HE DESIRE for spiritual nourishment was great in many parts of Europe, and movements of thought which gave intellectual content to what in so many ways was an inchoate search for God have their own dignity. Neither of these, however, comes first in explaining why the Reformation took root here and vanished there— why, in fact, this complex of anti-papal 'heresies' led to a permanent division within the Church that had looked to Rome. This particular place is occupied by politics and the play of secular ambitions. In short, the Reformation maintained itself wherever the lay power (prince or magistrates) favoured it; it could not survive where the authorities decided to suppress it. Scandinavia, the German principalities, Geneva, in its own peculiar way also England, demonstrate the first; Spain, Italy, the Habsburg lands in the east, and also (though not as yet conclusively) France, the second. The famous phrase behind the settlement of 1555—*cuius regio eius religio*—was a practical commonplace long before anyone put it into words. For this was the age of uniformity, an age which held at all times and everywhere that one political unit could not comprehend within itself two forms of belief or worship.

The tenet rested on simple fact: as long as membership of a secular polity involved membership of an ecclesiastical organisation, religious dissent stood equal to political disaffection and even treason. Hence governments enforced uniformity, and hence the religion of the ruler was that of his country. England provided the extreme example of this doctrine in action, with its rapid official switches from Henrician Catholicism without the pope, through Edwardian Protestantism on the Swiss model and Marian papalism, to Elizabethan Protestantism of a more specifically English brand. But other countries fared similarly. Nor need this cause distress or annoyed disbelief. Princes and governments, no more than the governed, do not act from unmixed motives, and to ignore the spiritual factor in the conversion of at least some princes is as false as to see nothing but purity in the desires of the populace. The Reformation was successful beyond the dreams of earlier, potentially similar, movements not so much because (as the phrase goes) the time was ripe for it, but rather because it found favour with the secular arm. Desire for Church lands, resistance to imperial and papal claims, the ambition to create self-contained and independent states, all played their part in this, but so quite often did a genuine attachment to the teachings of the reformers.

Hans J. Hillerbrand

MULTIPLE CAUSATION IN THE REFORMATION

Hans J. Hillerbrand, professor of history and Dean of the Graduate School, City University of New York, is one of the most prolific American

From Hans J. Hillerbrand, *Men and Ideas in the Sixteenth Century* (Rand McNally and Co., Chicago, 1969), pp. 24-33, 64-67. Reprinted by permission of Rand McNally College Publishing Company.

Reformation scholars writing today. His works include *Christendom Divided: The Protestant Reformation* (New York, 1971); *Men and Ideas in the Sixteenth Century* (Chicago, 1969); *A Fellowship of Discontent* (New York, 1967); and *The Reformation: A Narrative History Related by Contemporary Observers and Participants* (New York, 1964). Professor Hillerbrand currently serves as American editor of the *Archive for Reformation History.*

BUT EVEN this official pronouncement [the Edict of Worms] on the part of the German Empire did not settle the case of the heretic Martin Luther. Instead of suffering a violent death at the stake Luther was able to live out his life and die peacefully in bed. If we ask the reason for this surely unexpected turn of events, several answers suggest themselves. One was provided by none other than Emperor Charles himself when he remarked after his abdication that it had been the greatest mistake of his rule to have honored Luther's safe-conduct after Worms. There is a measure of truth in this reflection, for we can hardly overlook the powerful role played by the Wittenberg professor in subsequent events. But alone it does not suffice as explanation, for Luther actually was removed from the scene for almost a year following his dramatic appearance before the German diet at Worms and not a few people actually thought him dead. A far more incisive factor was the widespread and increasingly intense popular support for Luther. Here was not merely a "drunken German monk," as Pope Leo X had naively quipped, who had prompted the controversy, but a host of men who in a variety of ways made Luther's cause their own. They took to their pens and committed their thoughts to print. During the first years of the controversy Luther had borne the brunt of the literary battle; but as time went on he acquired numerous assistants. Not all of them were capable and most of them lacked creativity, but they all possessed a burning desire to further the cause of Luther—as they understood it.

Thus, Luther's word became print and indeed more than that: it became flesh, for from pulpits everywhere the Lutheran message resounded. Its spread was thereby vastly intensified. Catholic priests turned into staunch partisans of Luther. People throughout the land, listening to their preachers, no longer heard the proclamation of the old faith, such as they had known from the days of their youth, but a new evangel, new slogans, new doctrines, new principles. While the enormous circulation of Luther's tracts was an important means in spreading his message beyond Wittenberg, the contribution of countless ministers to the propagation of the new faith in the length and breadth of Germany was equally significant.

Within a few years Luther had found an army of devoted followers. The popular appeal of Luther's proclamation must not be overstated. That there was a response, at first vague and haphazard, then widespread and determined, is beyond doubt. But we must not assume that every man, woman, and child flocked to this new proclamation. Not everyone could read and acquaint himself with Luther's writings. And not all those who were able to read were interested in religious matters. In other words, we are speaking only of a limited segment of the populace—the intellectuals, the educated, the middle class—if an all-too-modern term is permissible—which must not be equated with society at large. Among these people support for Luther was extensive.

In part this support was due to a real commitment to Luther's religion, in part to an inadequate understanding of what he stood for. The fact is that Luther wore a coat of many colors: he could be seen as a German nationalist who asserted himself against Rome, as a humanist who echoed the concern for ecclesiastical change, as a social reformer who identified himself with the discontent with the existing state of society. The vagueness of Luther's early proclamation and the swiftness of the course of events made such divergent interpretations both possible and likely. If the papal nuncio Aleander reported from Germany in 1521 that nine-tenths of the people shouted "Luther," then one must not only question the numerical accuracy of his statement but also, and more significantly so, whether the people who so shouted knew what they were actually saying.

In short, Luther's cause had many strange bedfellows in those early years and the parting of the ways between Luther and some of his disciples which occurred later on was inevitable. But even afterward Luther's cause continued virtually unabated, an indication that it possessed real support. And this point must not be lost in overly sophisticated interpretations, for without the recognition that Luther's message somehow or other touched the religious feelings of his contemporaries we fail to comprehend his impact.

Luther confronted his contemporaries with a new interpretation of the Christian gospel, which, no matter how vaguely presented at first, proved sweetly attractive. Luther personalized religion, insisting that man's true service of God does not consist in the carrying out of externals, but in the free and spontaneous expression of faith. One might almost say that Luther simplified religion by advocating a religion based only on Scripture, only on faith with rules, regulations, theoretical distinctions dismissed as irrelevant. The Christian was called upon to put his trust in God. Religion was no longer complicated, no longer an oppressive external routine; it was faith.

At the same time, Luther made religion democratic. This is to say that he insisted that each individual personally apprehend and reflect upon the gospel. Luther's proclamation was the declaration of religious independence of the laity—of all those, in other words, who theretofore had stood on the sidelines and passively watched the religious pageant. When Luther placed a German version of the New Testament into

the hands of the people in 1522, he carried out in actual practice what he had already theoretically espoused. The willingness and ability of laymen, untrained in theology, to discuss religious matters with more learned opponents was a characteristic of the early Reformation. Hans von der Planitz, a Saxon councillor at the Nuremberg *Reichsregiment,* for example, ably defended Luther and on one occasion retorted to the charge that monks were leaving the monasteries because of Luther's teaching that there was nothing wrong with their leaving, for the early church had not known monks.

To the popular dimension of Luther's cause must be added another one. The Edict of Worms had transformed Luther's cause into a legal case. As a result of this, legal maneuverings increasingly came to the fore after 1521. The prime question was whether the Edict could be administered in the German territories in the face of the intense support for Luther. Or, if it could not, what kind of *modus vivendi* could be found for the adherents of Luther's message? Accordingly, the focus of the ongoing course of events was legal and governmental. In the three years after Worms, the *Reichsregiment,* the "imperial regiment" that took the Emperor's place in his absence from Germany, had to address itself to the problem, not so much in order to formulate policy, but to see to the execution of the Edict during the Emperor's absence. The efforts remained unsuccessful and afterward a long succession of German diets from Speyer in 1526 to Augsburg in 1555 grappled with the religious problem. Each of these diets faced it in a different form, though basically the question always remained the same: Should the Edict of Worms be administered or rescinded? Should the Lutheran proclamation be accepted?

Thus the character of events changed after the Diet of Worms of May 1521. What had been a theological controversy over the opinions of one individual turned into the Reformation. Nothing illustrates this better than the fact that Martin Luther, who had precipitated the tumultuous happenings, increasingly faded from the limelight and ceased being the central figure. Naturally, his spirit was still very much present, as was the awareness that it had been his theological thought that had brought about this searching, if turbulent, reformulation of the Christian gospel. But from then on the story of the ecclesiastical transformation may well be told without Luther, who was content to pursue his round of academic activities at Wittenberg.

The years after Worms were a time of storm and stress during which Luther experienced the resounding popular response and the exuberant group of disciples that made for a movement of vast dimensions. At the same time, those years were a period of clarification during which men sought to delineate more carefully the implications of Luther's message. Up to this point its statements and concerns had been broad, comprehensive, and general. Then came the second thoughts, the critical scrutiny, the searching reassessment. And not all saw eye to eye, and naturally the ways parted.

It began in the fall of 1521 in Wittenberg. Luther was still in the castle of the Wartburg, but at Wittenberg some of his impatient peers demanded that whatever practical changes were demanded by the new understanding of the gospel should be undertaken at once: if the Mass was unscriptural, its celebration should be stopped immediately. Since others inclined toward a more cautious procedure, tensions arose in the city and in the end only Luther seemed to be able to save the day. When he returned he took a stand against those who had advocated sweeping and immediate changes, arguing that externals should only be altered after the minds and hearts of the people had been changed. To effect ecclesiastical renewal by external fiat and by the introduction of new regulations was but another perversion of the gospel, no different from the existing practice. Moreover, Luther argued, the Christian faith knows not only rules but also freedom, and concerning some of its aspects no rigid rules exist. Luther advocated a reform at once conservative and modest. In the end it was this orientation that characterized the manner of ecclesiastical change in those places where his word counted.

A second parting of the ways came with the German peasant uprising of 1524/25. While the underlying causes for this uprising reach back into the fifteenth century and indicate, most of all, the uncertain place of the peasants in society, the grievances expressed by the peasants in 1524 had a new ring to them. They were clad in language taken straight from Luther's book—phrases like "the grace of God," the "word of God," "God's righteousness," which served as a kind of Lutheran embellishment to long-standing peasant concerns and demands. The peasants' most famous document, the *Twelve Articles* of 1525, demanded, for example, that ministers should preach only "the pure word of God" and be appointed by the congregation. They stated, moreover, that if any demand was found to be contrary to the Scriptures it would be disavowed. Luther had clearly made an impact on the peasants. As events were to show, however, the peasants were in for a profound disappointment.

The initially haphazard response of the authorities allowed the uprising to spread from its cradle in the southwest corner of Germany to South and Central Germany. At first the peasants' demands were moderate, and the possibility of concord existed. But it was not achieved. And this is the real tragedy of the uprising. As time passed, the peasants turned increasingly radical and the encounters with the forces of the rulers were marked by grim ruthlessness on both sides.

In the end, the peasants went down in defeat, for they were no match for the well armed soldiers of the rulers. As they went down, so did their hopes and aspirations, and so did Martin Luther whom many peasants saw as their mentor. Uncannily, the peasants' uprising had become part of the Reformation and a disastrous part at that. Luther had written two pamphlets dealing with the demands of the peasants, entitled *Friendly Admonition to Peace* and *Against the Murderous and Plundering Hordes of the Peasants.* The latter clearly sided with the authorities and smote with harsh words the peasants, who were to be "slain, stabbed and killed" by the rulers. Afterward Luther was chided for having been double-tongued in the matter, at first having encouraged the peasants and then siding with the authorities. Actually, he had been consistent throughout, always rejecting the use of religion for the realization of social and economic goals. In the first of his two tracts he had in truth sympathized with the grievances of the peasants, but had insisted, nonetheless, that social and economic matters had to be settled by the experts in secular fields, rather than by experts in the gospel. But Luther was not only convinced that using the gospel in pursuit of social and economic goals was theologically wrong. He was also persuaded that it would have no beneficial result. The uprising would lead to anarchy—and anarchy would produce more injustice and harm than had tyranny. It was a deeply sensitive man who faced the turbulence of the peasants' uprising, sensitive to what he saw as the mandate of the gospel and sensitive to considerations of prudence. This is, surely, the deep irony of his confrontation with those who sought alleviation for some of the most pressing social problems of the time.

Five years after the Edict of Worms no one could doubt that this document was a scrap of paper. It had proved ineffective. Luther, and the movement that he had precipitated, were still very much alive. Lutheran pamphlets continued to issue from the printing presses and Lutheran preachers continued to propound the new faith. Indeed, at more and more places this evangelical proclamation led to new forms of ecclesiastical life: different forms of the divine service were used and new structures of organizational life were developed. No longer did a single professor of theology alone proclaim a new version of the Christian gospel; a movement had emerged and assumed ecclesiastical form.

Naturally, such could not be done without the support of governmental authority. No matter how extensive the popular enthusiasm for Luther's evangel, if the territorial rulers had remained hostile, no empirical consolidation could have taken place. Such was the case for two reasons: firstly, the rulers considered themselves responsible, in one way or another, also for ecclesiastical affairs and, secondly, they were the ones called upon to administer the Edict of Worms. The second reason was crucial, since the unwillingness on the part of some rulers to administer the Edict allowed the new faith to expand. A telling expression of this state of affairs came at the diet held in Speyer in 1526, when the time for a resolute suppression of Lutheranism had seemingly arrived. The unanimous stand of the territorial rulers against the rebelling peasants suggested that at long last they might be willing also to put down the Lutheran heresy since rebellion and heresy seemed but two sides of the same coin. But it turned out that Lutheran sentiment was astoundingly strong and after lengthy deliberations the estates could not agree on anything but that each ruler should deal with the Edict of Worms— that is, administer it or not administer it—in the way he felt he could justify standing before God and the Emperor. This provision was meant as a truce, a temporary solution, for the return of the Emperor of Germany was presently expected and hope prevailed that he would bring the contested religious issue to an acceptable conclusion.

This temporary provision of 1526 determined the development that was to characterize subsequent German history: each ruler decided the religion in his realm. To be sure, another thirty years were to pass in Germany before this temporary provision was made definitive and the 1555 Peace of Augsburg legalized the ruler's right to reform. The path, however, was cleared in 1526.

Naturally, the question arises why some rulers were willing to embrace the new faith. Man being what he is, one suspects that concrete political advantages must have accrued from so doing. No doubt there is some truth in this and illustrations for ecclesiastical maneuvering for political advantages are not hard to find. The appetite may here well have come with the eating. . . . The place of the political authorities in ecclesiastical affairs had steadily increased during the fifteenth century and in the main the authorities possessed such power over ecclesiastical matters as they desired. But the religious controversy precipitated by Luther may have suggested to some that an opportune hour had come to usurp such ecclesiastical independence and prerogatives as still remained. At stake was not so much the ruler's intrusion in the inner affairs of the church, the way it believed and worshipped, but the numerous rights and prerogatives, both legal and financial, enjoyed by the church, which made it virtually a state within the state. This was the thorn in the flesh of the rulers, and the religious upheaval may have suggested a painless solution.

Some rulers, however, exhibited a genuine religious commitment. There were men who had been touched by the new evangel and their public policies were but the outward expression of their inner conviction. To uphold this conviction in the early years of reformatory change required a good deal of conviction. In later years the adherents of the Protestant faith enjoyed a measure of political and military stature which assured them safety; in the 1520s, however, the support of an outlaw and heretic was a touchy matter. When the Margrave of Brandenburg told Emperor Charles at Augsburg in 1530 that he would rather have his head cut off than attend Mass, he expressed his commitment to a religious cause. And even Landgrave Philipp of Hesse, youthful, impulsive, sensuous, politically concerned, gave evidence in those years of an authentic religious orientation.

The centrality of the territorial rulers meant the program of theological renewal advocated by Martin Luther became an affair of state, presented by governmental officials at official gatherings, by lawyers and councillors, by legal arguments and considerations. To be sure, while the lawyers and councillors did so at the gatherings of the German estates, someone stayed at home and kept the fires burning—ministers preached from their pulpits and counseled their flocks; theologians expounded the faith—and perhaps that was what counted. The formal decisions, however, were made elsewhere.

This political involvement of the Reformation led inextricably to political alliances and, in the end, to war. As early as 1524 several Catholic rulers agreed to form an alliance against the "damned Lutheran sect" and within a short time several Lutheran rulers had formed an opposing alliance. In 1528 came an illustration par excellence of the precarious state of tempers, when the maneuverings of one Otto von Pack brought the two camps to the brink of war. Pack had revealed to Landgrave Philipp of Hesse the existence of a Catholic plan to wage war on the Lutherans and Philipp promptly prepared for a defensive war in turn. As it turned out, the plan had been in Pack's head only, but Philipp's credulence indicated that a danger obviously existed.

The quest for a formal alliance of the adherents of the new faith reached its successful conclusion in 1531 with the founding of the League of Schmalkald, comprised of those Protestant territories and cities willing to accept the Augsburg Confession, the statement of faith submitted by the Lutherans at the Diet of Augsburg in 1530. No matter what its weaknesses, and there were several, this League proved an important factor in German politics for almost two decades. It was the political embodiment of Protestantism in Germany and its existence left little doubt but that any attempt to solve the religious question would have to reckon with this alliance.

The 1530s and 1540s brought one attempt after the other to resolve the religious problem. Whenever a diet met, it addressed itself to the issue, but each time with inconclusive results. This state of affairs allowed the Protestant faith to expand and to consolidate, for as long as the religious problem remained unsolved the Protestants were able to breathe freely and faced no difficulties.

The failure to solve the problem had several reasons. In the first place, a great deal of vagueness prevailed concerning the real issues that kept the two sides apart.

Were they certain ecclesiastical practices, such as the withholding of the communion cup from the laity or the celibacy of the clergy? Or was the divergence theological in nature, such as a different understanding of the sacraments or of the church? Today these questions can be easily answered; then, uncertainty and even confusion prevailed which made for haphazard and difficult situations.

A second point is closely related. Men on both sides, such as Melanchthon and Bucer among the Protestants, Gropper and Contarini among the Catholics, found the unity of Christendom an important consideration and declared themselves unwilling to face a schism. Their ecumenical sentiment propelled the efforts at conciliation forward from one attempt to the next and this delayed the eventual showdown. But both sides also had their more rigid and less conciliatory protagonists, men such as Eck and Luther, and these were more influential.

Last, but not least, there was a political consideration. Only one man might have been able to secure uniform ecclesiastical practice in Germany—the Emperor, who by virtue of both his temperament and his office thought it his responsibility to look beyond the confines of the individual territories and be concerned about the Empire at large. Charles V was prepared to exercise this function. Indeed, from his youth he had dreamed of his role as the guardian of Christendom, had aspired to recreate the empire of Charlemagne and rule over a domain on which the sun would never set, where all men would live in peace and harmony in the true Catholic faith. . . .

The real question in any study of the religious and ecclesiastical upheaval in the sixteenth century is how a purely theological phenomenon such as Luther's proclamation of salvation by grace was so widely and successfully translated into empirical realities. But this is a misleading question. From the very onset of the Reformation controversy the issue was not solely a religious or theological one, since extraneous factors played important roles in the course of events. Albert of Hohenzollern could not

view Luther's ninety-five theses as an exclusively theological pronouncement. Important political and financial considerations impinged on the matter and made him, by all odds, a prejudiced participant in the assessment of Luther's theological assertions. Or take the uprising of the German peasants in 1524/5, which indicated how easy it was to relate Luther's teaching to long-standing economic and social grievances. Then there is Henry VIII, who broke with Rome mainly over a personal problem and dissolved the English monasteries because of his financial difficulties. Even the key figure in the attempted suppression of the Lutheran heresy in Germany, Emperor Charles V, did not devote all his attention to the problem nor utilize all his resources against it, as he had threatened to do at Worms in 1521. He had other fish to fry and this diffusion of interest was to be of great significance for the course of events.

Thus, the Reformation always was a bundle of factors, political, social, and economic as well as religious. There were instances when factors other than religion were more prominent, even though the official pretense was piously religious. But in other instances authentic religious factors determined and oriented the events. Surely, we would not have expected the situation to have been different. Hordes of sinners turning into saints in a society singlemindedly concerned about religion . . . such is hardly a very realistic picture of the time. Some sixteenth-century folk may have been more religious than their ancestors or their posterity; most of them, one suspects, were not.

The non-religious factors that influenced the course of the Reformation in Europe have already been mentioned in the preceding chapter, but deserve to be recounted. The increasing importance of the ruler in the affairs of the various European commonwealths must be cited first, for this included a more powerful voice in ecclesiastical matters, even before the Reformation or in countries that remained Catholic. Accordingly, the distribution of power between church and state was undergoing a steady readjustment in the early sixteenth century, with an almost inevitable build-up of tensions between the two parties. In the German cities some burghers made a persistent effort to obtain a greater voice in municipal affairs, with a concomitant quest for constitutional changes. Then there was the struggle between France and Spain that consumed so much attention and energies during the first half of the sixteenth century.

Nor must one forget the Turks. Next to the persuasive eloquence of Luther's pamphlets the Turks were probably the best aids of the Protestant cause in Germany, and this in a twofold way. Firstly, the possibility of a Turkish attack upon Western Christendom so frightened the Emperor that he was willing to make important concessions to the Protestants at several crucial occasions in order to receive their financial and military support against the Turks. Secondly, Charles actually had to take to the field against the Turks in 1532 in Hungary, and three years later in North Africa. These occasions diverted his attention from the German religious problem long enough to give the Protestants in Germany another breather or to allow the pope to stall the convening of a general council yet a little more. Undoubtedly the course of the Protestant Reformation in Germany (and elsewhere) would have been a different one had there been no Turkish menace in the East.

The point of these reflections is that the Protestant reformers sought not only to propagate the new faith as widely as possible but also to achieve its formal recognition. In this effort they were aided by a variety of non-religious factors. Since religious pluralism was generally unthinkable in the sixteenth century, such recognition had to come from the political authorities and entailed the repudiation of the established Catholic religion. Initially the Protestant reformers may have entertained fond hopes of having their proposals for ecclesiastical reform incorporated into the fabric of Catholic life and thought. But after the harsh realities of the controversy had shown this to be an impossibility, they strove for the official acceptance of the new faith in the place of the old.

At that point two possibilities emerged. One was an immediate or early Protestant success, and thereby the introduction of the Reformation. This happened in Saxony, Hesse, in numerous imperial free cities in Germany, and in England (if here one does not apply the term Protestant too meticulously). The second possibility was a prolonged Protestant struggle for recognition. Such was the case in France, Scotland, Poland, or wherever the ruler did not forthwith accept Protestantism and officially introduce it as *the* religion in his realm. Accordingly, an effort had to be made to attempt the official introduction of the Protestant faith against the will of the ruler or to force him to make the change. Both situations had in common that the ruler played the central role.

Thus, the fact that a certain territory became Protestant meant nothing more, on the face of things, than a decree of the political authorities that the Protestant religion was thenceforth to be the official one. Naturally, such official introductions themselves said nothing about the sentiment of the people, but were acts of state with varying degrees of popular support.

That people in large numbers *did* embrace the Protestant faith can be safely asserted; this fact constituted the prime reason for the persistent impact and success of the Reformation. Naturally, we would like to know the reason for their action and those among us fascinated by the insights and methodology of the social sciences will inquire about possible patterns of this change of religious allegiance. If such a pattern of ecclesiastical change does exist, it is difficult to discern. Only one comment may be made safely: people became Protestant (at least outwardly) whenever their ruler commanded them to do so. Otherwise, the situation is rather confusing: some of the clergy turned Protestant and others remained Catholic. Some of the nobility turned Protestant, others remained Catholic. Some artisans decided one way, some the other. In Germany the peasants rallied around Luther, while in England and Sweden they rose up in arms on behalf of Catholicism. It would be fascinating if all humanists, all academicians, all the educated (or all the uneducated), all the rich (or all the poor), all those in authority (or all those desiring authority) had become Protestant. But there is no such neat evidence, at least not so far as the general picture is concerned. What can be said is that the Protestants were generally the younger generation, outside the intellectual and ecclesiastical establishment. While this is admittedly a modest observation, it is the only one that may be made legitimately—except for the more obvious one that those concerned about religion were the most likely candidates for conversion to the new faith.

III. THE REFORMATION IN A CHANGING SOCIETY

Basil Hall

THE REFORMATION CITY

In the Holy Roman Empire most cities adopted some form of the Reformation. In addition, many urban centers in various parts of Europe proved more receptive to the new ideas than did the rural populace. Basil Hall, professor of ecclesiastical history at the University of Manchester, has analyzed this phenomenon to ascertain the roots of movements which threatened an established society.

IT WOULD be well for us to take up Hamlet's purpose to "go back to school in Wittenberg," and set aside the "truant disposition" of his fellow student Horatio, who left Wittenberg behind him. For to think of Luther without his city is a not infrequent fallacy. He who talks about the Reformation must begin with Wittenberg since it was there that Luther began and maintained the Reformation. All subtleties of definition on what we mean by the Reformation, on the historical importance of the earlier beginnings and later deviations of other men besides Luther who were inspired by the need for reform in the Church, cannot set aside that fact. The Protestant Reformation, which began and developed in Germany, showed the closest interrelation of religious movement and urban environment: for that matter the origins of Protestantism were everywhere urban. The first victories of Luther's theology up to 1525 were achieved as a popular movement within towns, especially in the free cities of the Empire. The successful rise of early Protestantism took place, for example, in Bugenhagen's Hamburg and Lübeck, Spengler's Nürnberg, Oecolampadius' Basel, Zwingli's Zürich, Bucer's Strasbourg—and, later, Calvin's Geneva. Anabaptism, which was regarded by the Reformers as a fanatical attempt to overthrow the barely established reformed Churches by a parasitical invasion of their cities, in one of its forms won and shattered the city of Münster. But the implications of the fact of the essentially urban environment of the Reformation seem to have attracted too little attention from historians. . . .

We tend to make the economic and political history of the sixteenth century separately identifiable from the thought forms of the men who experienced that economic and political life. But in the sixteenth century religion was essential to the ways in which men expressed political ideas, social judgements, and economic practices: to separate the political, social and economic from the religious in that age is difficult and when attempted can be misleading. The religious and the secular were not divisible. Some sixteenth-century European men may have disliked the Church of Rome or the Churches of the Reforma-

From Basil Hall, "The Reformation City," *Bulletin of the John Rylands Library,* vol. 54 (1971), no. 1, pp. 103, 105-113, 115-118. Reprinted by permission of the John Rylands University Library.

tion or hated the clergy of either, but they were not therefore secular-minded or irreligious, and they clothed their political, economic and moral views in religious terms, not because they had no other language for them but because they wanted to do so. It is misleading to describe the religious views of Luther on *Obrigkeit* in modern political terms to accommodate a Harold Laski; or to describe Calvin's religious view of banking practice at Geneva in terms appropriate to the sociological or economic viewpoints of a Max Weber or an R. H. Tawney. This can lead to entanglements from which such writers seek to extricate themselves by distorting, if not weakening, the careful balance of judgement which Luther or Calvin had maintained. This should not allow us, however, to take the easier road of writing on the theologies, the liturgies, the Church structures of Luther and the Lutherans, Bucer, Zwingli and Calvin, as though these were ends in themselves, without reference to the changing environment of the cities where revolutions took place which made possible the expression of those themes and which helped to mould their differing patterns. We should give more attention than is usual to examining how the theologians of the cities of the Reformation experienced limitation in the conditions of the environment of their cities as well as a fruitful stimulus for new developments; how they sought religious sanctions for political change; and how they made the cities into propagandist strong-points for counterattack on resistant Catholicism.

The very close interplay of these factors is clear from the large correspondence of all these men: it springs out vividly from their pages. Yet their correspondence is frequently neglected by those who write on the Reformers, for writers find it easier to discuss a Reformer's theological treatise uncluttered by political, social or economic limitations than to analyse the historical contingencies in his letters. It was environmental pressures which helped to divide Luther from Zwingli, as well as differences in temperament and in theology. When Luther faced Zwingli in debate at Marburg in 1529 the current of hostility could leap between them even from their differences in speech: Luther, the royalist High German of the Empire, found Zwingli's Swiss German to be speech appropriate to what he regarded as the religious fanaticism and the dubious republicanism of the Swiss Confederates. For Luther afterwards Zwingli was not just *schweizerisch* but *schwetzerisch*. This is no excuse, of course, for falling into the trap of making religious themes the product of environmental determinism. I myself strongly maintain the independence and vitality of the thought of the Reformers, and I do not intend to modify it in accordance with preconceived views on the social and economic structures of the period. Whatever hesitations you may have about the possibility, or the usefulness, of the study I propose, you will agree that regardless of the environment, in the last resort those powerful theologians of the great Reformation cities vigorously asserted the truth as they saw it, in spite of what princes, bishops or city magistrates might propose. Nevertheless, they did not live all their lives at the extreme stage of "in the last resort," but in the ongoing life of their cities, which pressed their theologies into new moulds; and it is in that context that I wish to discuss them.

Let us then "go back to school in Wittenberg," which was the backdrop of the Lutheran drama, and not only to *Lutherstadt Wittenberg*, but also let us go to Lübeck, representative of the Northern cities and of the dying political power of the Hanseatic League: to the golden city of Augsburg, centre of the Fuggers, where it was said a Scottish king could wish to have been housed as nobly as one of its patricians: to Nürnberg, where Dürer's eye saw life with a new religious realism yet a city cautious, conservative and always loyal to the Emperor: to Strasbourg, tolerant of many varieties of religious belief, home of the politically and religiously radical guilds, especially the stormy guild of gardeners of which even Bucer was a guildsman: to Basel the university city of the humanist Reformer Oecolampadius and the chosen home of

Erasmus, who died there protesting against its Protestantism: to Zürich, where Zwingli, a prophet in arms, made a civic community into a Church and died for his city as a good Confederate should: to Geneva, the Savoyard city, where dice-playing swordsmen made a revolution and captured to serve them a young and reluctant Frenchman, Calvin, who made them the not always willing servants of his *civitas Dei.* And also we should go to school to Ulm, Regensburg, Hamburg, Constance and Memmingen, and to the city of the blood-stained saints, Münster. If we did so we should glimpse a great variety of constitutions and of city councils, political associations, economic and social life, in a bewildering range of patterns, in which it is dangerous to generalize from one group to another. Each city had its particular characteristics and the contrasts between them are sometimes extreme. There was nothing in common between, for example, the political, cultural and economic life of Wittenberg and of Geneva. We must distinguish between the conservative Northern imperial cities, the more intellectually and socially lively Southern imperial cities, and the cities of the Swiss Confederation which had only a shadowy relation to the Empire. Geneva was not even Swiss but Savoyard and therefore associated with the Empire. Strasbourg had no tradition comparable to the fierce Swiss independence of Zürich, and it had no large cantonal region from which it could draw a ferocious and ready manpower like Zürich and Berne, from whose villages, as from those of other cantons, came the mercenaries who fought in most major European conflicts on either side in the period up to the battle of Marignano in 1524. But Strasbourg, because of increasingly weak episcopal control in the fifteenth century, had won not only independence, but also through its able statesmen, a most liberal and balanced constitution which was much admired by Erasmus and other humanists. Basel more than any of the other cities, not excluding Augsburg and Nürnberg famed for the arts, was the spiritual home of many Northern humanists. It was the city where

Erasmus chose to return to end his days, in spite of its Protestantism, in doing so rejecting Oxford, Cambridge, Louvain, and Paris, where he could have triumphed: but they lacked free air, they were not free cities. However, the Northern imperial free cities had no universities, no humanists, no Swiss republicanism, and they settled for a conservative Lutheranism and did not deviate from it. The Northern cities differed for the worse from the Southern in their degree of intellectual liveliness. The South German imperial cities, on the other hand, through their political needs as well as developing intellectual trends were influenced by Zwingli's Zürich.

All these major centres are sufficiently different to make generalizations dangerous, but, allowing for the different economic and political settings, all these cities wanted greater expansion and social change and in all of them religious reform was an initiating or contributing factor in that expansion and change. Nevertheless, these centres of social experiment and intellectual vitality were doomed to lose their initiative and much of their freedom by the middle of the sixteenth century. They lost their leadership and the drive behind the renewal they sought, through the increasing pressure of Charles V (relying no longer as at first on the appeal to imperial unity, but on his Spanish and Flemish resources in men and money), and through the princes of the Empire, who saw in the cities an undesirable independence of mind and political life. One by one, with the exception of the Confederate cities of Basel and Zürich, though these were also constricted, they lost their effective freedom of initiative and were assimilated to the neighbouring power-structure of an Elector, prince or duke. Because of its distance from these forces in the Empire only Geneva survived in independence along with her allies the Swiss.

The upsurge and decline in the dynamic energies of the cities came in the period 1450-1550. This is equally the period of the upsurge of the Northern humanist and Reformation movements and of their later loss of dynamism. By 1550 had come the full development of the national power structures of Spain, France, and, of the lesser nations, England and the rest, whereby the medieval concept of the democratic and free city as an independent political unit was lost. Even Zürich and Geneva had by that time come to resemble on their small scale the nation-state ideal of the politics of the period in which political freedom and social experiment were considerably limited. But in 1450 only the most astute of statesmen in the Empire would have grasped how great a change in the status of the free cities was to come. To understand that upsurge of energy in the cities after 1450 already mentioned we should remember the origins of the sense of corporate identity in the city. The free cities of the mid-fifteenth century had grown from the medieval city. The medieval city had grown because *Stadtluft macht frei*: men did not build their city walls to shut in serfs. Men moved into the medieval town to win a measure of freedom, and to find variety in place of the monotony of labour in the fields, for in the town they found taverns, the continually moving spectacle of street life, and the great churches with their popular preachers. In the towns men found community; not least, if they could acquire the skills, they could enter the community of brotherhood in the guilds. If a man was ambitious, or young and hopeful, he came to the towns for opportunity—though only a very few of the immigrants could become Dick Whittingtons, yet still they came. (It has been calculated that nearly 50 per cent. of the population of the Netherlands in the sixteenth century were town-dwellers.) Like Gray's frustrated peasants, the majority of citizens were poor, and "chill Penury repressed their noble rage." Bread riots were endemic, but this at least added stimulus to town politics.

Special opportunities had come to the towns in the early thirteenth century when many towns became almost independent states. From this period grow two kinds of towns in Germany (and the distinction is important), towns of the Empire, *Reichstädte,* which could develop into free cities, and territorial towns, *Landstädte,* which

were subjected to a lay or ecclesiastical prince: it was the *Reichstädte* which became free cities which are important. By the fifteenth century the free cities of the Empire were struggling against interference from neighbouring princes, or against the resident bishop. This was because until then they had been comparatively free from interference; since until about 1350 the energies of the German princes and knights had been taken up by opposing or fighting for the Emperor, in either case to establish or extend their own territories.

In their struggles for freedom the imperial cities became the most efficient and planned political structures in the German Empire. The cities kept chronicles, records of their transactions and council decisions—this literacy meant a stimulus to education in which laymen could share, for within the city walls it had become no longer the exclusive monopoly of Churchmen. This literacy meant the historical awareness of precedent, and of the means of constitutional change, and of political expertise. The economy of the cities was a planned economy, subject to control, in which merchants had to proceed according to statute. But capital could and did accumulate, a fact dangerous for the survival of the democracy of the guilds in the fifteenth century, which was to be supplanted in so many cities by the oligarchy of patrician merchants. Cities developed their own laws and from the fourteenth century onwards were bringing in jurists familiar with Roman civil law, which in most cities came to be combined with the local or territorial law. This brought a greater sophistication in the administration of the law in the cities compared with the more cumbersome procedures of the countryside and of the princely courts; and again provided a field for the educated layman. Further, the cities, through their trade, developed an international awareness; when merchants corresponded with foreign cities on the state of trade their horizons in more ways than one were enlarged. This internationalism brought with it diplomatic skills, and also, another sign of increasing political sophistication, espionage, in the watch kept on strangers at the inns. Police organization, night watchmen, and other ways of social control were characteristic of the cities in notable contrast to the lawlessness and brutality of the countryside. Doctors and midwives were appointed and salaried by City councils. Cities had their regulations on extravagance in dress, licentious behaviour, gambling, prostitution, the punishment of insults to religion, including work on Sundays. Even the attitude to begging, regarded as an opportunity for Christian good works, changed in the cities, since townsmen thought hard work a sign of the good life. For example, Strasbourg in the later fifteenth century clamped down on its hordes of beggars, and insisted that those wholly incapable of work should be registered and made to wear a distinctive badge. More efficient taxation systems were evolved to pay for and to manage all this. Military service was demanded for the protection of the city and grew to something much more significant than a mob of armed citizens. The patrician lords of Nürnberg, for example, took knightly arms for their shields and banners, raised their troops, and gave money for cannon foundries which provided the famous artillery of that city.

Cities expanded their territories, ensured that the villages in their orbit gave them food and soldiers, and provided them with protection in return; however, this expansion was restricted by the jealousy and vigour of neighbouring princes, one reason why the pattern of the Italian city-state did not develop in Germany. Another area of expansion in the life of the cities was found in that most enduring and self-governing medieval institution, the Church, which was brought in several ways under the authority of city councils. Because of the influence of the clergy on political and social matters, city magistrates intervened in ecclesiastical affairs: here they followed the example of the princes in concerning themselves with the appointment of abbots and, where cathedral chapters contained canons belonging to prominent patrician families, sought to influence episcopal elections. They even nominated priests for benefices. They con-

trolled ecclesiastical building: the soaring spire of Strasbourg cathedral was begun under the care of the citizens whose magistrates controlled the fabric. The secularization of Church property in closing religious houses where this was thought to be desirable was well under way a century before the Reformation, which in this respect no more than completed a process already begun, by wholly rejecting the religious life. Moreover, in the fifteenth century anti-clericalism was marked in all imperial cities, as it was in the towns in general. The struggle for power between citizens and bishops of all episcopal towns had been a constant factor of medieval life, and in the fifteenth century many bishops temporarily or permanently left to reside outside of the city walls to avoid the frequent disturbances. By the early sixteenth century only the Archbishop of Cologne succeeded in holding to his status within his city. As part of the background to these attitudes to the Church we should remember that the Church owned, it has been suggested, nearly one third of all the land in Germany.

One aspect of this city life is particularly important for our purpose, and that was the sense of a corporate identity among citizens. You belonged to your town not only visibly by residence but invisibly in a mystical sense of identity with it. When you took your vow of citizenship at moments of peril in the city, it was as serious as baptismal vows and with a similar sense of mystical identification. The German imperial city held its citizens as the Jews of old had been held by Zion. Sin or blasphemy by individuals was not only against the glory of God but could destroy a city like the invasion of disease could destroy an organism. How significant this idea could be for developments in the Reformation period should need no emphasis, especially at Zürich and Geneva, which survived the loss, or great curtailment, of political independence experienced by the German imperial cities.

The development of a city council, it is also obvious, was of fundamental importance for the self-government and sense of independence of the citizens. Where a council began to develop, it meant that there was a conscious aim of the citizens to win political control for themselves, for example, at Geneva from the prince-bishop; and the composition of a city-council reflected the power pressures of different social groups. Many cities had a patrician class whose families were alone capable of electing members of the council, which became a self-perpetuating oligarchy. But other cities either cast out the patrician group, as, for example, at Basel, won control for the guilds, or made a compromise which was effected by the admission of new members to the patrician class, at the same time appointing guildsmen to one or more of an increased number of councils. There was tension here between the pressing forward by the craft guilds and the resistance of the patrician merchants who tried to close the ring against them. This tension was further stimulated by the renewed growth of population in the fifteenth century, which in turn raised new pressures through the increased development of industry and commerce. . . .

Into this situation Martin Luther burst forth with challenge after challenge, between 1517 and 1521, to the structure of the Church, to the traditions of dogma and worship, to the accepted notions of the nature of society and of men's relations to each other in it, and leaving men bewildered as to where he would break out next. All this came not from a new Savonarola, a prophet of righteousness, nor from a Taborite preacher of fanaticism and war, but from a highly professional professor of biblical studies in the recently founded university of Wittenberg, a position which he held throughout his life. Not the least part of the extraordinary quality of Luther's reformation was that it should have come from remote and shabby Wittenberg and not from a great and well-known city like Nürnberg, Lübeck or Strasbourg. Wittenberg was not a free city of the Empire, and it did not even have a German name, for it had originated with Flemish immigrants in a region which was not even ethnically German but Wen-

dish. It is true that it was the residence of the Elector of Saxony, Frederick the Wise, who, ashamed of its appearance, had undertaken a great building programme between 1490 and 1509 to improve its appearance and amenities. In that period he completely rebuilt the castle, the castle church, the town-hall or Rathaus, in Renaissance style, and in 1502 founded the university, and rebuilt the Augustinian house in which Luther came to live as a friar. But contemporaries were not impressed. Cochlaeus, Luther's able Catholic opponent, described Wittenberg in the twenties as "a miserable poor dirty village in comparison with Prague." But then he was not comparing like with like. Even Luther's friend Myconius (though he was not a native son) could describe it as more like an old village than a town. But the peak of exasperation with remote and shabby Wittenberg was achieved by Duke George of rival Ernestine and Catholic Saxony when he said: "that a single monk out of such a hole should undertake a reformation is not to be tolerated." Wittenberg was a town far removed from the possibility of comparison with Strasbourg with its soaring cathedral tower, from the patrician splendour of Augsburg or Nürnberg, from the pomp and dignity of the Hanse cities, from the humanist culture of Basel, and from the vital energies of the guildsmen of Zürich.

The great creative ideas were being tested first within the house of the Augustinian Eremites and within the walls of the university, but when they moved out into the pulpit of the castle church, and in the form of the Ninety-five Theses on Indulgences in German translation published in the streets, the ordinary man was roused and pressed forward to hear more about this freedom of grace which cut through a tangled undergrowth of prohibitions, superstitions, and financial exactions for priestly services. When he also learned that there was no distinction between a priest and a layman and that all baptized Christians were priests of God, then he held a new political weapon in his hand. For the last forty years most writing, by Catholics as well as by Protestants, has been directed to the theological development of the young Luther. That this intensive study has been most fruitful and indeed has transformed not only Luther studies but also studies of the intellectual origins of the Reformation cannot be doubted. But it has not been accompanied by an equally thorough study of the social and political energies of the early Reformation years, which saw such vigorous activity stirred up by Luther's message.

Luther was like someone who dynamites an old house to clear the way to build a new one, without thinking of the effects on adjoining properties, and is then astonished to see how many more houses come tumbling down—for Luther's teaching was immensely explosive, to his own surprise, at just that period of time and in that country. Luther had never intended what occurred during his enforced absence in the Wartburg after the Diet of Worms in 1521, the sharp radical trend of Karlstadt's innovations at Wittenberg, where Melanchthon trembled before the prophets of judgement from nearby Taborite-influenced Zwickau who were stirring the citizens to new heights of excitement. It was the Elector who called a halt to this millenarian trend, and Luther himself had to return to restore order, realizing slowly that he must adjust the balance disturbed by his own earlier teaching on the freedom of a Christian man. For it had proved to be heady teaching to ordinary townsmen to learn that there was no distinction between a priest and a layman and that all baptized Christians were priests of God. What had been lacking for many a frustrated Savonarola or Hans the Drummer, from the fifteenth century up to Luther's time, was now, it seemed, available: here at last was a theological justification for change in political structures which were so intimately linked with ecclesiastical structures. Protestant historiography, especially where it has been associated with the traditions of Lutheranism in church life and practice, has drawn the picture of a cautious conservatism in the Lutheran preachers and their princes who brought a gradual change from one ecclesiastical structure into another and more effective one, and then drawn a further picture which showed that social radicalism was the work of the Zwinglians and the Calvinists. According to this view, Lutheranism was essentially concerned with scripture and grace, and it was the Swiss who added a more radical social programme to their theological purposes. This is, of course, true, but it leaves out too much, and therefore it blurs the actual situation. First, the troubles at Wittenberg in the winter of 1521-22 were a paradigm of what could happen elsewhere, and secondly, the concentration of attention on Luther's theology of grace is too exclusive. Luther not only *coram Deo* through biblical study, *Anfechtungen* or trials of faith, and his great skill in the techniques of that Scholastic theology available to him, rediscovered the Pauline doctrine of grace but also, without his originally intending it, let loose powerful forces opposing the structures of the visible Church of his time. Luther had wanted to talk about the justifying grace at Leipzig and Worms in 1519 and 1521 but John Eck, and other opponents, forced him on to ground from which he had to challenge papal authority and the totalitarian authoritarianism of curia and hierarchy, who used councils and canons in support of that authoritarianism. Luther's new theology, in the eyes of both intellectuals and of ordinary men, was not only splendidly setting forth *sola scriptura* and *sola gratia*, it was also consequently seeking new ways of organizing men's lives, in giving a new and simpler pattern to ecclesiastical structures and in making their society more amenable to their own control. Therefore, *sola gratia* and *sola scriptura* were instruments by which men who sincerely believed in them found release from the sense of restriction under complicated controls which seemed antiquated and frustrating. The Reformation ran across the Holy Roman Empire, across the German Reich, from city to city like a sweeping flood, in this great territory lacking centralized royal power. When it faced much better organized and centralized monarchical states like France, Spain and England, or the Catholic nationalism of highly sophisticated societies like those of Northern Italy, it slowed down: its only hope was that the prince could accept it or tolerate it, or alternatively its leaders could prepare for a martyr's struggle. We hardly appreciate enough how intense for so many ordinary townsfolk was their anti-clericalism, their powerful dislike of the ecclesiastical system which touched their lives at so many points and, they felt, too often with ill-effects. Townsmen felt that they must have greater freedom of social and political action to obtain improvements in economic affairs and in the administration of justice.

Peter J. Klassen

THE ROLE OF THE MASSES
IN SHAPING THE REFORMATION

Currently serving as Dean of the School of Social Sciences at California State University-Fresno, Peter J. Klassen is a professor of history and former department chairman. His publications include *Europe in the Reformation* (Englewood Cliffs, 1979), *Church and State in the Reformation* (St. Charles, 1975), *The Economics of Anabaptism, 1525-1560* (The Hague, 1964), and various articles.

FEW ASSUMPTIONS concerning the Reformation in the Empire have been so unhesitatingly asserted and so widely accepted as the view that political establishments determined local responses to the Reformation. Generations of historians have perpetuated the view that the Reformation was "imposed from above." Many scholars speak of the "magisterial" Reformation in which the magistracy is regarded as the decisive factor. Government officials are seen as those who shape policy and implement it; the citizenry as a whole is of little consequence. The magistracy, whether in the person of a territorial prince, city councils, or territorial ecclesiastical princes, was sufficiently powerful to determine which religious changes, if any, would be adopted in a particular city or territory. A typical expression of this viewpoint is found in the Reformation volume of the *New Cambridge Modern History:* "The Reformation maintained itself wherever the lay power (princes or magistrates) favored it; it could not survive where the authorities decided to suppress it." Similarly, a prominent American Reformation specialist has written: "Only one comment may be made safely: people became Protestant (at least outwardly) whenever their ruler commanded them to do so." Such conclusions continue to characterize a large part of Reformation historiography.

Many contemporary Reformation historians take this assumption for granted. If there is any doubt, a quick reference to *cuius regio, eius religio* is surely more than adequate to persuade the hesitant. Owen Chadwick, in his Pelican *History of the*

From Fred Schroeder, *Five Thousand Years of Popular Culture* (Bowling Green State University Press, Bowling Green, 1980). Reprinted by permission of the Bowling Green State University Press.

Reformation, regards the decisive role of the temporal power as beyond serious question. "Throughout the Empire, from Hamburg in the north to Zurich or Geneva in the south, the cities easily accepted the new doctrines and their councils easily undertook the reform and supervision of the parishes." The questions of why city councils undertook such action, or what role the citizenry played in decision-making, however, are left unanswered.

Other historians have depicted the Peasants Revolt as a major turning point as far as the significance of popular opinion is concerned. Under the leadership of Thomas Müntzer and other champions of the peasants, thousands of the poor rose against their oppressors, usually the local landlord. The poorly-led and ill-equipped armies of the peasants proved no match for the military forces of the lords, and soon the revolt was drowned in a sea of blood. The consequences of this violent upheaval have long been debated. Some historians have argued that the bitterly disappointed peasants now turned against Luther and his reformation. They had learned that the will of the masses counted for little. Similar conclusions have been expressed by various Marxist historians. One of the recent writings of a historians' "collective" in the German Democratic Republic depicted Luther as having provided an opportunity for the exploited peasants and the town laborers to rise against their oppressors, but by 1523 the "peasant-plebeian masses" were being deserted by him, for he had drawn ever closer to the territorial princes and the emerging capitalistic bourgeoisie. When the populace learned that Luther's religious reformation could not be used to effect a social revolution, Luther and his reformation lost their popular appeal. A new champion of the exploited poor appeared: Thomas Müntzer now led what the late Soviet historian M. M. Smirin described as a "people's reformation." Then, with Müntzer's defeat, according to the German Marxist Alfred Meusel, the reformation movement was narrowed to "a reformation of the princes."

Such sentiments are, of course, by no means limited to Marxist historians. Widely-used textbooks have perpetuated the idea that, after the Peasants Revolt, Lutheranism ceased to have "broad class support." Similarly, James Mackinnon spoke for many when he wrote that with the defeat of the peasants, "Lutheranism ceased to be a popular creed," while one of the most prominent Reformation historians writing today contends that after the Peasants Revolt, the "Magisterial Reformation in Germany stood with the princes and patricians."

The early Lutheran movement has, of course, always been recognized as having gained broad popular support. Cardinal Aleander's frequent references to the popular clamor for Luther are a fair indication of the alarm felt by many contemporaries. But such popular support has not generally been regarded as a decisive factor in shaping Reformation policies. Recently, an increasing number of scholars have come to insist that townsmen and peasants have been underestimated as participants in the drama of that age. Studies such as those of Bernd Moeller, Franz Lau, Helmar Junghans, Gerhard Seebass, Max Steinmetz and others, have supplied an overdue corrective. Further examination of archival sources is needed to determine the extent to which popular opinion actually forced the hand of the magistrate, and why the populace acted as it did. In numerous instances, the magistracy vigorously opposed the Reformation, yet it was introduced and established. Popular pressure was often a decisive factor, both before and after the Peasants Revolt. Obviously, the administrative machinery of the political establishment was used as the vehicle for change, but such action was often the result of coercing the magistrates. In some instances, where magistrates refused to respond to popular pressure, they were summarily removed from office.

Instances of popular pressure prevailing over the wishes of the magistracy are numerous. At the same time, they are clearly not universal, and so generalizations about the decisive role of the peasants or the townsmen are dangerous—just as sweeping assertions about the all-powerful role of the magistrates are inaccurate. It must be re-membered that the Germany of Reforma-tion times was composed of scores of politi-cal entities, such as independent principali-ties, imperial free cities, and ecclesiastical territories. Political structures varied from substantially democratic to virtually abso-lute, from essentially independent to the largely subordinate. No formula fits all situations in this mosaic, and no uniform policy of responding to the challenge of the Reformation is to be found. But two con-clusions can be safely made: towns and territories did not become Protestant or remain Catholic simply because their princes or town councils told them to do so, nor did the populace respond only to any one specific stimulus.

Some indication of the significance of popular opinion is suggested by the exten-sive efforts put forth to shape that opinion. Avalanches of pamphlets and broadsides were often loosed upon communities, while persuasive orators addressed crowds in city squares and elsewhere. Often, the popular movements generated their own forms of expression and expansion, as is demon-strated by the numerous ballads and folk-songs which swept the crowds along. Illiter-acy was not so great a barrier to propaganda efforts as might be expected, for the car-toons of the broadsides often told the story as compellingly as any treatise. Beyond that, public orators, or readers to assembled throngs, further mitigated the problems of illiteracy, while the emotions generated by the songs of the time needed no written expression. Clearly, the masses were subject to manipulation by many elements, but that did not mean that their aroused sentiments, however biased or ill-informed, were incon-sequential in shaping events. The sixteenth-century towns and villages were often swayed by crowds who were aroused and, in their excitement, determined to control their destiny.

It must, however, not be assumed that the victory of popular pressure necessarily meant the triumph of pro-Reformation forces, either before or after the Peasants War. On more than one occasion, the reten-tion of the traditional faith represented a victory for the sentiments of the citizens. The imperial free city of Rottweil presents an interesting case study for the conflict of popular movements. Here the Reformation made substantial inroads so that at the Diet of Nürnberg in 1524 the Cardinal legate Campeggio warned that Rottweil was *luther-anissimo*. Nonetheless, when a pro-Refor-mation communication from Constance was delivered to the city council, the council threw the messenger in the tower. As ten-sions mounted, the council tried to preserve peace by expelling leaders of both sides. Yet such a measure failed to stop the agitation, and the city divided into two hostile fac-tions. In July and August 1529, civil strife threatened to break out into the open, for champions of both positions held public rallies, and numbered their supporters in the hundreds. Archduke Ferdinand warned the city that, unless decisive action were taken, the imperial Hofgericht would be transferred from Rottweil, thus depriving the city of a significant source of income and prestige. But such economic pressure did not quiet the populace. Finally, the council invited the peasants in the surrounding villages, which were under Rottweil's jurisdiction, to come into the city to help resolve the issue. These peasants did not share the widespread feeling of anti-clericalism and were strongly in favor of the old religion; consequently, that faith now enjoyed a clear majority position. Thus reinforced, the council ordered those who refused to support the traditional faith to leave the city. As a result, 60-100 families left the city. Rottweil, in response to pres-sures of the majority of townsmen and peasants, had remained Catholic. Emperor Charles, in gratitude for this action, sus-pended the city's imperial financial dues for fifteen years.

In several other imperial free cities such as Buchau, the Reformation movement never gained a significant following, so that no popular pressure was necessary to retain the old faith. Sometimes, as in Heilbronn in the 1520s, strong popular agitation for, and vigorous public defense of, both Catholic and Lutheran positions neutralized the power of the citizenry and allowed the city council to direct affairs, but only until one side gained a convincing majority. In other centers, such as Rottenburg on the Neckar, strong popular support kept the city Catholic.

Many of the Northern towns similarly adapted their religious practices to popular pressure. In Osnabrück, a Hansa town as well as the seat of an archbishop, champions of both positions carried their cases to the citizenry by means of public debates. A contemporary chronicler noted that Lutheran teachings gained strong support and were introduced into all the churches except the cathedral, and that this was done "without the approval of spiritual or secular authorities."

A reluctant council continued its struggle, but gradually pressures from the "common people" forced the authorities to sanction changes they had been unable to prevent. At least to participants in the struggle, the outcome demonstrated the very real power of the citizenry, quite apart from the wishes of the authorities.

The decisive role played by the "common man" *(der gemeine Mann)* is also illustrated in the case of Goslar. Despite repeated attempts to maintain the traditional position, the city council in 1528 admitted that refusal to bow to public clamor would mean the outbreak of revolt. The resolute opposition by the Bürgermeister led to his being forced from office, and the Reformation movement, pushed by the "miner and the common man," compelled the magistrates to bow to the popular will. A similar trend of events occurred in Bremen, Soest, Lüneburg and Herford; in each instance, the city councils resisted change, but were compelled to permit the introduction of Lutheranism when pressure from the populace proved too strong.

Few towns so clearly demonstrated the power of an aroused populace as did Lübeck. Here, champions of the Lutheran position often interrupted religious services by singing the widely-recognized symbol of Reformation zeal, *Ach Gott, vom Himmel sieh darein.* A determined council, however,

vigorously resisted change, so that tensions between it and the citizenry steadily mounted. After several confrontations, matters reached a crisis on December 10, 1529. A crowd assembled on the city square and demanded that the council appoint Lutheran ministers. The council refused, and when a spokesman for the populace asked those who were prepared to "live and die according to God's Word," to raise their hands, members of the throng did so. The council was forced to capitulate; two Lutheran preachers were appointed.

But even this retreat proved inadequate, for the citizens soon demanded that the mass be abolished throughout the city. Again the council resisted. The townsmen were warned that to carry out such a policy would have dire consequences; besides, why not await decisions of the imperial diet? Once again the citizens refused. A beleaguered council finally yielded, and agreed that a formal Reformation should be introduced. Johann Bugenhagen was accordingly invited to direct the Reformation of the city.

In the city of Halle, ecclesiastical and political rulers cooperated to prevent the introduction of the Reformation, but their efforts failed. The city was under the jurisdiction of the Archbishop Albrecht of Hohenzollern, who attempted, from his residence in the Moritzburg, to direct the affairs of the city. With the defeat of the peasants in 1525, the archbishop was able to consolidate his position, but only temporarily. Lutheran tendencies again asserted themselves, and Albrecht responded by removing some of the council members. At the same time, he enlisted the support of his brother, Elector Joachim I of Brandenburg. These two were joined in an alliance with Duke George of Saxony, Duke Erich of Braunschweig-Kalenberg and Heinrich of Braunschweig-Wolfenbüttel. Despite such a formidable alliance, Archbishop Albrecht could not halt the growth of Lutheranism in his city. When the citizens elected pro-Lutherans to the city council, Albrecht declared that he would rather have "a small Christian, obedient council than a large one composed of opponents of the old religion," and banished those councillors who supported Lutheranism. This was in 1539; two years later he had to admit that he had lost the struggle. Now, he was prepared to strike a bargain: if the city would accept new taxes, he would withdraw his opposition to religious change. The council presented this proposal to the citizens, and found the townsmen ready to accept an added financial burden in exchange for religious self-determination. Accordingly, the archbishop was given his added revenue, while the people were permitted to have their new religion. Albrecht soon left the city and ensconced himself in the more hospitable environment of his archiepiscopal seat in Mainz.

Developments in some of the small territorial and city states were often complicated by the influence of more powerful neighboring states. Thus, when the Reformation gained some support in Hildesheim, bishop and council opposed the change. A determined minority of the city thereupon approached the ardently Lutheran Philip of Hesse, and enlisted his support for its cause. Faced with the threat of intervention by Philip and his allies, the city council decided to bow to the inevitable and introduce the Reformation. An external threat had proved decisive—and such tactics were by no means unusual, and were used both by Catholics and Protestants. When the small county of Ortenburg, an independent principality but surrounded by Bavarian territory, adopted Lutheranism, the duke of Bavaria used military force to restore the old religion. Similar tactics were used by a resolutely Lutheran prince in the case of Gnoien when Duke Johann Albrecht used military force to introduce the new religious order. Not infrequently, however, developments in the smaller principalities were determined by internal factors. In the county of Baden, the local lord, Heinrich Flackenstein, was vigorously and successfully resisted when he attempted to prevent religious changes in Weiningen.

In Ortenau, Count Wilhelm von Fürstenberg found that the new teachings could not be regulated or stopped by his decree. Again, when authorities in the county of Lippe tried to halt the growth of Lutheranism, they found themselves unable to cope with the situation, and had to yield to popular pressure. On the other hand, official policy in the county of Haag favored Lutheranism, but a determined populace forced the retention of the old faith. Similarly, in many of the large and important cities, such as Strassburg, Nürnberg, and Augsburg, councils adopted the Reformation because of "pressure from the populace."

At the same time, powerful rulers, as in Bavaria, the two Saxonies, and Hesse, were often the decisive element in either maintaining the old religion or establishing the new. Such instances demonstrated effective political organization, or, not infrequently, a lack of popular support for the Reformation. Historians have too often forgotten the substantial number of people in the Empire who had no desire to change the religious system.

The refusal of the populace simply to be a passive bystander while the political establishment decided official religious policies is further demonstrated by the various efforts put forth to worship in accordance with specific beliefs. Frequently, a persistent pro-Catholic segment of the population went to considerable lengths to maintain the old religion, and was fully prepared to accept the added inconvenience of going to a nearby village or town in order to hear the traditional mass. Thus, when the Reformation was introduced in Frankfurt, parishioners who remained faithful to the old religion went to mass in nearby Bockenheim. And when the Reformation was introduced into Tübingen, adherents of the traditional position went to mass in neighboring Lustnau. Similarly, when Lutheranism triumphed in Schwäbisch Hall, many townsmen made the added effort to go to mass in a nearby church.

Neither Catholics nor Protestants were prepared simply to bow to official policies. Thus, when George, Duke of Saxony, vigorously opposed Lutheranism, some of his subjects such as the peasants of Annaberg and/or the townsmen of Leipzig undertook journeys of several hours' duration in order to worship as they wished. Even expulsion of some offenders did not bring a uniform religious policy. Ironically, in electoral Saxony, Frederick could see no reason why he should dispose of his relics and thus deprive himself of an important source of revenue. Only reluctantly did he yield to popular demands and remove the relics.

Conditions in the peasant parishes around Ulm (but within the territorial jurisdiction of the city) are a good indication of continued devotion to Catholic practices, even in areas which had vigorous pro-Reformation forces. When the city council learned of numerous parishioners who went to mass in nearby villages, an extensive survey was ordered. Some of those interrogated declared openly that they could not give up their old faith, no matter what the personal or economic consequences. An examination of the court records demonstrates that Protestants had no monopoly on a willingness to suffer for their faith. Nor were these adherents of the traditional position content to accept the decisions of the city council. Clearly, both Catholics and those who became Protestants were often united in their belief that religious faith was not simply to be based on decisions reached by the political authorities.

Towns, whether imperial free cities or territorial cities, afford especially many instances of decision-making by non-magisterial elements in the population. The imperial free city of Reutlingen presents an unusually clear picture of the power of the populace as opposed to that of the magistracy, and may serve as a case study. Here Matthäus Alber, the champion of Luther's teachings, gained a significant following. By 1523, the situation had become sufficiently alarming to unite the Bishop of Constance, the Swabian League and Archduke Ferdinand in their determination to prevent the growth of heresy.

In September 1523 the Hapsburg authorities in Stuttgart warned Reutlingen that unless appropriate action were taken, Württemberg would implement an economic boycott of the city. The city council responded by denying the charge of heresy, but at the same time, professed a readiness to take corrective action, should any proof of the allegations be forthcoming.

When Archduke Ferdinand reiterated the charges and, in addition, the Swabian League warned of the danger of heresy, the city council determined to clear itself of the charge. Alber would be sacrificed for the well-being of the city. The council requested the Bishop of Constance to hold a hearing in Reutlingen; the bishop agreed to send his vicar, Dr. Johannes Ramming. Aware of the popular support enjoyed by Alber, the city council tried to counteract this potential threat by appealing to the guilds for support. The guilds, however, refused this request. In a memorable meeting in the town square, they insisted that the council change its position. There would be no hearing for Alber unless a similar process were initiated against "the small and the great councils, or the entire citizenry (Gemeinde)."

Faced by the solid opposition of the citizenry, the city council reversed its position. Popular pressure had proved stronger than the will of the council. At the insistence of the assembled citizens, the Bürgermeister and council were forced to join the citizenry in a common vow to "remain with the pure word of God." Popular agitation carried the day against formidable political pressure.

Archduke Ferdinand was not to be easily dissuaded, and on September 18, 1524, ordered all his subjects in Württemberg to have no contact or business dealings with Reutlingen. Yet even so drastic a measure failed to alter the determination of the Reutlingen citizenry. Even the threatened military intervention of the Swabian League moved the city only to adopt a more conciliatory position, but not to abandon its Lutheranism.

Variations of the Reutlingen procedure are to be found in numerous other centers of Reformation activity. In the important imperial free city of Ulm, Lutheranism gained an early following, so that by 1522, the city council was arresting and imprisoning those suspected of holding to the new teachings. The city fathers were convinced that the peace and order of the city were threatened by a movement which drew its support from the "common man." After several years of efforts to halt a movement which many viewed as being potentially seditious as well as heretical, the city council finally submitted to pressure, and referred the issue to the citizenry. Almost 2000 citizens were entitled to vote on the matter; 87 percent supported a Lutheran position. Faced with such a decisive verdict, the council moved to implement the wishes of the citizenry.

In Constance, popular sentiment early became a decisive—and coercive—factor. When an imperial representative attempted to proclaim the edict against Luther, a crowd gathered on the market-place and prevented his doing so. When a local priest, Johann Wanner, became a champion of Luther, Bishop Hugo of Constance in 1524 tried to remove him from his position and bar him from further priestly activities. The city council tried to comply, but finally had to admit that they could not control events; Wanner continued to preach.

Other centers experienced similar popular pressures. In Coburg, pressure from the citizenry had become so strong by 1524 that the city council decided to yield. In Mülhausen, the monk Heinrich Pfeiffer launched an incendiary attack on the religious establishment, and gained an enthusiastic following as early as 1523. When the council tried to take action against him, a threatening crowd persuaded the authorities to desist. The Archbishop of Mainz urged action, and the council again tried to devise an arrangement which would avoid radical change. The crowd responded by presenting the council with a series of demands (July 3, 1523). Faced with a determined citizenry, the council capitulated but the concession had come too late. An aroused citizenry soon forced the council members to vacate their offices, and a new council was chosen.

Despite the numerous instances which demonstrate the power of popular pressure, it is apparent that often other factors proved decisive. In some instances, military assistance from anti-Lutheran forces proved more than adequate for maintaining the old order. Thus, when the Reformation movement gained a strong following in Schwäbisch Gmünd, the city council resolutely tried to halt the growth of the new movement. In 1524, some representatives of the citizenry presented a written request for the appointment of a Lutheran minister, but the council informed the petitioners that the local priests had already been instructed to preach only the "pure Gospel." Such responses proved unacceptable to the advocates of change, and pressure continued to build. Eventually, the Swabian League intervened militarily to maintain the position of the city council.

Several years later, pressure for change had again become so intense that the city council could maintain itself only by getting military help from the Hapsburg Statthalter in Stuttgart. Repeated appeals for external military assistance (coupled with a vigorous anti-Lutheran drive spearheaded by the city's Franciscans) eventually allowed the council to break a popular movement.

In some instances, city councils avoided confrontation with the town populace by referring crucial issues to the citizenry. Thus, in 1529 the citizens of Biberach were asked to vote on the position the city should take relative to the protest of Speyer. A large majority voted for the Lutheran position; magistrates who opposed this action were forced out of office. Similarly, when only 142 of 1076 enfranchised citizens of Esslingen voted against the introduction of Lutheranism, the city council moved to accommodate the demands of the majority.

Sometimes the city council was slow to recognize the power of an aroused citizenry, as in Memmingen. Here the council at first opposed the growth of Lutheranism. In July 1523, when a group of citizens urged the city council to make concessions to Lutheranism, the council resisted. As pressure for a reformation mounted, champions of the traditional position warned the council not to submit to the demands of the "common man," but the opponents of change, including the Bürgermeister, found themselves forced out of office. Thus, when the city council moved too slowly to implement the demands of the citizenry, a public demonstration in summer, 1524 again compelled the council to conform to popular pressure. Sweeping Lutheran practices were introduced early in 1525. The populace had scored a clear triumph. Shortly thereafter, in the turmoil of the Peasants War, the Swabian League intervened to restore traditional practices, but by late 1525 a Lutheran minister had again been installed. External pressure and the defeat of the peasants had not deterred the citizens in their resolute drive to establish Lutheranism. Later, when the city had to take action relative to the Edict of Speyer, the city council referred the issue to the citizenry. When 751 of 812 voting citizens supported the Lutheran position, the council acted accordingly.

It should be noted that, although magisterial authorities were often compelled to carry out the wishes of the populace, the magistracy ordinarily still remained the channel through which citizens implemented their decisions. But the crucial factor in these instances is that the town councils or other authority figures were not the locus of decision-making; they were the instruments of the will of the populace, whether townsmen or peasants. Thus, the assumption that the response to the Reformation challenge may be expressed simply in terms of the "magisterial Reformation," one in which the political authorities determined what action was to be taken—must, in many instances be rejected or modified. Often, city councils or princes were forced to take action against their will; citizens, far from being passive, were often vigorous and decisive proponents of the new—or of the old—religions. Their motivations cannot be explained by any simple mono-causation. Economic, political, social and religious factors were usually so thoroughly intertwined that the role of the populace may not be viewed as only a struggle for economic justice, or political rights or religious freedom. In many instances, of course, the military might of a prince crushed popular agitation, yet often the will of the people maintained itself, and decided whether a region would become Protestant or remain Catholic. And once a decision had been made, the minority, whether Protestant or Catholic, further asserted independence from the authorities by often refusing to attend the established church services, by enduring persecution, or by emigrating. In any event, the populace may not be dismissed as being inconsequential in determining the course of the Reformation in Germany nor may the significance of either material or spiritual factors be ignored.

Imogen Luxton

THE REFORMATION AND POPULAR CULTURE

Movements as pervasive as the Reformation were certain to have a powerful impact on popular culture. Imogen Luxton, formerly a research scholar at the Institute of Historical Research in London, is now a

From Imogen Luxton, "The Reformation and Popular Culture," in Felicity Heal and Rosemary O'Day, eds., *Church and Society in England* (Archon Books, Hamden, Conn., 1977), pp. 59-61, 68-77. Reprinted by permission of the Shoestring Press.

principal in the Department of Education and Science in the United Kingdom. Her essay examines religious change and its reflection in society, and notes that significant trends in popular literature were part of the Reformation legacy.

THE MAIN characteristic of provincial culture at all levels before the Reformation was its predominantly religious content. Few secular works occur in lists of books in wills or inventories. The secular literature written in provincial England before the Reformation emanated from three main sources: monastic antiquaries interested in the history of the founders of their religious houses; town clerks turned antiquaries such as Robert Ricart who wrote *The Maire of Bristowe is Kalendar;* and noble families such as the Stanleys, earls of Derby, who continued to inspire in the north-west midlands the neo-feudal loyalties on which the ballad tradition flourished. In the west midlands there was one notable exception to this pattern of secular literature in the writings of a member of the Cheshire gentry, Humphrey Newton of Pownall Hall, whose poems comprise one of the few collections of formal secular lyrics that survive in manuscript for the early sixteenth century. The majority of his compositions are in the Chaucer—Lydgate tradition of courtly love poetry from which they borrowed subject matter, motifs, images and vocabulary. They also reflect the continuing influence of a regional alliterative tradition which dated back to the 1350s when the alliterative revival of the fourteenth century developed and flourished in the west midlands and borders.

The continuing influence of later medieval religious traditions can be seen in the mystery plays which appear to have enjoyed support up to and beyond the Reformation, although becoming increasingly archaic in their literary form. In the west midlands and borders whole cycles were performed at Chester and Coventry while individual Corpus Christi plays were performed at Worcester and, according to a bequest in a local will, at Tamworth in Staffordshire too.

Corpus Christi pageants were also performed at Hereford. Traditionally it has been thought that the plays were presented in a processional manner before a large audience. This view has been challenged as far as the Chester cycle is concerned and the theory of a stationary performance advanced. More recently, it has been suggested that the Chester plays were performed indoors before a limited audience rather than mass gatherings. The popular character of the Coventry plays has not, however, been disputed. The plays seem to have been presented at several stations in the town and they attracted "very great confluence of people thither from far and near."

Although the surviving texts of the Chester cycle and the two extant Coventry plays represent late versions of the plays, they exemplify the main features of late medieval religious culture. The essence of the play cycles was the presentation in simple, colourful and dramatic form of the scriptural narrative, ranging from the Old Testament stories to the nativity, the missionary life of Christ, his passion, resurrection and ascension. Legendary material which had grown up around the scriptural texts was uncritically presented alongside the biblical stories, while the human characterisation in many of the plays contributed a humorous element. The latter did not detract, however, from the high religious tone of the plays, whose major themes were the redemption of mankind and, reflecting late medieval eschatological preoccupations, the day of doom. The plays thus epitomised a predominantly image-orientated culture in which the basis of the Christian faith was presented visually and, in some cases, through a cloud of legends and myths. The impact of the plays is illustrated by the example of an old man whom the Yorkshire divine John Shaw came across in 1644 in

Lancashire. Although the old man claimed to be a regular church-goer, he maintained that he could not recall ever hearing of salvation by Jesus Christ except in a Corpus Christi play which he had seen at Kendal "where there was a man on a tree and blood ran down." His comments indicate that the impact of the plays was predominantly visual but that the message of the Scriptures left some imprint on uneducated minds.

Other forms of popular religious drama were the performances of the Christmas mummers; the unveiling of the Rood in churches on Palm Sunday; and the resurrection from the Easter sepulchre on Easter Day, through which the themes of birth, death and rebirth respectively were dramatised. The presentation of Christian doctrines in visual form was also the purpose of a number of half-secular ceremonies which flourished on the fringes of the Christian year. Among these was the custom of the boy bishop which had grown out of both the cult of St Nicholas and the pagan feast of the Saturnalia and which involved the dressing up of children, one of whom was chosen to bear the title of bishop, and their participation in some of the services of the church for the space of one or more days between St Nicholas's day and the feast of the Holy Innocents. Bequests in a number of local wills of scarlet gowns for the use of the boy bishop in St Michael's Coventry and Ludlow testify to the continuing popularity of the ceremony in parts of the west midlands in the early sixteenth century. The ceremony retained considerable secular content and, indeed, in Bristol was the occasion of some festivity, but it was countenanced by the church because of its instructive value in showing that God himself had been made incarnate and lived on earth as child and man. Through these religious or semi-religious observances, which were concentrated in the six months of the year between 24/25 December and 24 June inclusive, the whole life of the community was pervaded by the pre-Reformation church. . . .

The development of popular Protestantism in provincial England and particularly in the north and west of the country was slow and localised. In the west midlands and borders it made most headway in Bristol and Coventry where there was an old tradition of religious dissent which, in the case of Bristol, had been fuelled on the eve of the Reformation by the activities of a local bookseller, Richard Webbe, who sold and distributed religious works proscribed by the government. In Bristol the pulpit became the scene of open controversy between the supporters of the new faith, led by Hugh Latimer, and defenders of the old, led by the eccentric preacher Hubberdyne. In the course of three sermons delivered at Bristol during Lent 1553 Latimer preached against pilgrimages, the worship of images, and the abuse of masses and pardons and it was reported to Cromwell that "many in this town are infected by him, from the highest to the lowest." Again in 1559 there was a disturbance in Bristol caused by the visit of the Scots reformer, George Wishart, who was alleged to have gained many converts by his preaching, and in that year depositions about heresy in Bristol were taken by a royal commission set up to investigate sacramentarianism. In Coventry, too, Protestantism succeeded an earlier Lollard tradition. According to Thomas Lever, writing to Bullinger in 1560, in Coventry "there have always been, since the revival of the gospel, great numbers zealous for evangelical truth."

Elsewhere in the west midlands and borders and, as Christopher Haigh has shown, in Lancashire also, Protestantism before the accession of Elizabeth developed as a predominantly academic movement. It was implanted by local men, converted at one of the universities, who returned to their native counties to convert their families and friends and, in the case of men such as the Lancastrians John Bradford and George Marsh, to attempt to spread the new religion through their preaching. Small, closely-knit circles of Protestants were formed such as that which Thomas Becon encountered in Warwickshire in the early 1540s and which consisted of Hugh Latimer, John Olde and "divers other, whereof some were men very godly learned in the laws of the most highest and professors of the same" who were engaged in godly studies. With the exception of a brief period during Hugh Latimer's episcopate at Worcester, however, there was little attempt by any of the local clergy to follow up the proselytising activities of the visiting preachers. In 1551, in his *Homilies on the Romans* printed in Worcester and addressed to the clergy of his diocese, Bishop Hooper lamented that the majority of the people were still ignorant of God's word. Throughout the sixteenth century Protestantism had to contend with the persistence of long-standing traditions of superstition on the one hand and popular scepticism and indifference on the other. Thus in 1579 in his dedication of his translation of a discourse by Bullinger on the authority of Scripture, John Tomkys of Bilston, Staffordshire, who was appointed perpetual preacher of St Mary's Shrewsbury and a town preacher in 1582, complained that there was no shire, city or town and almost no household which was not poisoned either by superstition or by atheism (by which he meant irreligion).

The Reformation, however, did have an immediate impact on many aspects of customary life. The shrines and relics which had been the focal points of local cults were systematically destroyed and the old ceremonies and rituals abrogated. The vicar of Much Wenlock in Shropshire, for instance, recorded in his register the burning on 7 November 1547 of the bones of St Milburgh (on whose burial site had stood the priory of Much Wenlock which was surrendered in 1539) together with the images of St John the Baptist from nearby Hope Bowdler; St Blaise from Long Stanton; Mary the Virgin from Acton Round and another image of the Virgin Mary. While the tone of the vicar's entries reflects his sympathies for the old order, like the great majority of the clergy and laity he conformed outwardly to the religious changes. Indeed, throughout the west midlands and borders iconoclasm and the introduction of Protestant forms met with little outright resistance. Even the protest of a townsman of Worcester against the removal of the shrine of the Virgin in Worcester Cathedral was inspired not by religious motives but by concern that the city would be deprived of a source of income from the flow of pilgrims to the shrine.

Devotional attitudes were not, of course, changed overnight and the old rituals lingered on, particularly in the more remote parts of the country. In Lancashire, where traditional practices survived on a larger scale and recusancy proved far more extensive than in Cheshire, a group of seventeen preachers drew up a report in 1590 on the religious condition of the county, in which they gave details of the popish fasts and festivals which continued to be observed, particularly at funerals, marriage ceremonies and baptisms. Moreover, superstitious customs persisted in ceremonies such as that at Rogationtide which the Protestant reformers had attempted to purge of its medieval associations and restrict to a perambulation for the purpose of beating of the parish boundaries. In the archdeaconry of Stafford in 1561 it was still necessary to charge the inhabitants "to avoid superstition and such vain gazing as they used the last year and in no case that they use either cross, taper, or beads, nor women to go about but men."

In other parts of the country, however, old traditions of Lollardy and popular heresy stimulated the spontaneous development of hostility to the ritual observances of the late medieval church. The activities of Matthew Price and his group of friends in Gloucestershire in 1539, for example, reflected the continuing influence of old traditions of popular radicalism which inspired contempt for the customary rituals. Holy water was held up to particular ridicule by Price, who was alleged to have sprinkled some in Upleadon church on William Baker of Staunton, who proceeded to turn his back in mockery of the ceremony. The services of matins, evensong and burial were also the objects of Price's scorn, as was the sacrament of penance which provoked his comment that "it was as good to confess him to a tree, as to a priest." Holy oil came under attack from William Bowre and William Cloterboke of Slimbridge, Gloucestershire, in 1549 when they are alleged to have said that it was "of no virtue but rather it is meet to grease sheep and boots."

The Reformation had a destructive impact not only on the ritual observances of the late medieval church but also on half-secular ceremonies such as that of the boy bishop, which was abrogated by royal proclamation in 1541, and on civic ceremonies. In Coventry the amalgamation of the Corpus Christi gild with the Trinity gild in 1535 and their subsequent dissolution in 1547 led to the alteration and later abolition of the St George's Day, Ascension, Whitsun and Corpus Christi processions, while in Hereford it was agreed in 1548 that the different crafts should contribute yearly a certain sum of money to be used for the benefit of the city in place of maintaining their usual pageants on Corpus Christi Day. The mystery plays survived in Chester and Coventry until the 1570s, although towards the end they were performed irregularly. By 1575, when the Chester plays were performed for the last time and in face of opposition from the archbishop of York and the Lord President of the North, it was recognized that some of the plays would have to be omitted "which were thought might not be justified, for the superstition in them."

The destruction of religious shrines and images and the abolition of the confessional left a vacuum in many people's lives. By undermining the healing power of saints' relics and images as well as the protective power attributed to holy words and consecrated objects, the Reformation deprived men and women of the prospect of supernatural aid which could help them with the problems they encountered in their daily lives. Nor was the established church of the Protestant reformers able to provide adequate substitutes to take their place in the lives of the majority of the uneducated. It is impossible to know whether, as a result, the demand for popular magic increased. Certainly, the cunning men appear to have retained their popular appeal in post-Reformation England. Moreover, the number of cases involving popular magic re-

corded by the church courts reached its peak under Elizabeth, but this may have been due to increased vigilance and efficiency on the part of the courts rather than to an upsurge in demand.

The Reformation did, however, give a fillip to the doctrine of divine providence as an explanation of and consolation for earthly misfortune. This teaching can be traced in popular broadsides in which national disasters were interpreted as manifestations of God's displeasure and in tracts such as Bishop Hooper's *An Homelye to be read in the tyme of pestylence,* printed in Worcester in 1553, in which he explained that the plague was the product not of chance or the influence of the stars but rather of divine displeasure at man's transgression. He urged that the remedy was for the clergy to bring the people to the knowledge of God's word. Unusual happenings in the natural world were seen as portents of things to come. A tract entitled *True News out of Worcestershire,* 1598, for example, listed recent prodigies which had been sent by God as admonishments to men to reform their lives. These included "sliding of grounds, removing of highways, mighty floods by great abundance of rain, fearful lightnings and thunders, great fire from heaven, sudden earthquakes, strange and deformed children born, great dearth of corn, mighty plagues and pestilence." As the schoolmaster of Olveston, Gloucestershire, explained in a tract following the terrible storm over Olveston in 1605, the faithful had no need to be dismayed by such events since they knew that the storm came from God: it was only those who did not know and acknowledge God who had cause to be terrified. The pious Christian could take comfort in the knowledge that no harm could befall him unless God permitted it, and could look forward to the prospect of eternal happiness as compensation for the trials of this life.

In place of the ritual and magic of the medieval church the Protestant reformers emphasised the sovereignty of God and the importance of the word as the source of faith. The parish clergy were urged to become better educated so that they could fulfil their preaching role and proclaim the Gospel for, as Bishop Hooper recognized in two tracts and in his visitation articles and injunctions of 1551, the growth of scriptural knowledge among the parochial clergy was a prerequisite for the development of the new faith among the laity. Like Archbishop Holgate of York in his injunctions for York minster of 1552, Bishop Hooper sought to impose on the clergy a programme of self-education based on the vernacular Scriptures. This objective was pursued throughout the Elizabethan period through visitation injunctions and through systems of exercises involving regular meetings of the clergy whether organized on the initiative of the bishop, as in the diocese of Chester under Bishop Chaderton, or on that of the puritan clergy as in the diocese of Coventry and Lichfield.

The evidence of wills and inventories indicates that there was a marked increase in book-ownership among the parish clergy in the Elizabethan period. The wills or inventories of 387 non-cathedral clergy in the west midlands and borders, proved between 1558 and 1603, have been examined and of these 150 or 39 per cent mentioned books compared with 31 per cent in the period 1490–1558. The ownership of Bibles, in particular, became more widespread; of the 40 wills or inventories which mentioned specific books, 17 mentioned the Bible. A study of these books mentioned by name reveals a distinct move away from the late medieval preaching-manuals and pastoral guides which figured so prominently in the earlier period but which were mentioned in only three of the clerical wills or inventories in this area during the Elizabethan period. Their place was taken by the theological works of the church Fathers and the leaders of the Reformation. Scriptural commentaries by continental reformers such as Wolfgang Musculus, Augustine Marlorat, Rudolph Walter, Calvin and Bullinger were owned by ten of the parish clergy in the area and books of sermons by Hugh Latimer and the puritan preacher Henry Smith were also mentioned. Most of the libraries were small although there are a handful of cases of

clerical libraries numbering 50 books or more and an exceptional case in 1610 of a library of some 370 books left by the vicar of St John's in Bedwardyne, Worcester.

By the end of the Elizabethan period, therefore, many of the parish clergy appear to have been better equipped to preach the word of God than their predecessors. The Protestant reformers' ideal of the minister actively engaged in studying the Scriptures and carefully preparing his sermons can be seen in the notebook of Robert Dobbs, vicar of Runcorn, Cheshire, 1580–1621. This contains notes under such headings as the eight benefits of the passion of Christ; the nine rocks which hinder perfection; the five ways in which God manifests his will, all of which are supported by biblical examples and references. In addition, Dobbs's extensive notes on predestination reveal his interest in the controversy within the church over that doctrine. Dobbs started by presenting the strict Calvinist doctrine of the total sovereignty of God and of each man's predestination to eternal salvation or damnation by the will of God. Like a good scholar, he then set out the counter-arguments, only to refute these by reference to the Scriptures.

While the clergy continued to be the main source of religious knowledge for the majority of the laity, the availability of the English Bible made it possible for literate laymen to obtain first-hand knowledge of the word of God through personal study of the Scriptures. The gradual growth of Bible-ownership at all levels of society can be traced in wills and inventories. Those proved in the west midlands and borders during Elizabeth's reign reveal that Bibles were owned by some 20 of the gentry as well as by a Bristol merchant, 3 yeoman, 1 husbandman and 7 men who were tradesmen or artisans.

As early as the 1540s there is evidence, albeit fragmentary, of the tremendous impact which the availability of the Bible in English was to make on the laity. According to Roger Edgeworth, prebendary of Bristol from 1542, the English Bible found enthusiastic readers among the Bristol merchant community. In one of the series of sermons which he preached on the gifts of the Holy Ghost towards the end of Henry VIII's reign, he observed:

> I have known many in this town, that studying divinity, hath killed a merchant, and some of other occupations by their busy labours in the Scriptures, hath shut up the shop windows, fain to take sanctuary, or else for mercery and grocery, hath be fain to sell godderds, steanes, and pitchers, and such other trumpery.

Elsewhere in the west midlands and borders there are a handful of cases of men of humble circumstances reading the vernacular Bible in the 1540s. In the case of Humphrey Grynshill, a weaver of Stonehouse in Gloucestershire, his action in reading aloud from the English Bible in Christ Church, Gloucester, in April 1541 and declaring that masses for the dead were worthless, because there was no scriptural authority for purgatory, provoked a public disturbance of the kind which led to the passing of the 1543 Act prohibiting the reading of the Bible among the lower orders.

The impact of biblical study on the religious knowledge of the laity can be seen too in the arguments advanced by a number of the Marian martyrs. While the offending statements of the Bristol martyrs, for example, reflected old traditions of popular radicalism, others of the martyrs demonstrated an ability to handle theological issues. Thus, knowledge of the biblical texts made it possible for John Careless, a Coventry weaver imprisoned for his faith during the reign of Mary, to hold his own in the course of his interrogation on such difficult questions as predestination and the concept of the elect church.

Biblical study was further stimulated by puritanism which developed in the west midlands and borders in towns such as Bristol and Coventry which had been most receptive to Protestantism and in the eastern pastoral area of Chester with its growing trade and industry. The Bible was at the heart of puritan preaching and, in puritan households such as that of John Bruen of Bruen Stapleford in Cheshire, texts were memorized by those who could not actually read them. One of Bruen's servants, Robert Pasfield, while unable to read or write, had not only memorized the Scriptures but had developed such an understanding of them that he was "a godly instructor and teacher of young professors."

Although direct evidence is lacking, it seems reasonable to conjecture that the availability of the Scriptures in English and Protestant emphasis on direct study of the texts may have stimulated the diffusion of literacy in sixteenth-century England. Literacy itself in the sixteenth and seventeenth centuries can only be measured statistically in terms of the ability of men and women to sign their names. The Cambridge Group for the History of Population and Social Structures are currently investigating the extent of literacy defined in this basic way. The role which writing and, more particularly, reading played in the ordinary life of local communities is not susceptible to measurement in statistical terms. It can only be assessed on the basis of contemporary statements such as that of the Chester herald and poet, Thomas Chaloner, who commented in a poem written in the 1570s that those verses addressed to the farmers were written in vain since "the farmer meddles not with looking out of books."

If books played little part in the life of the farming community, evidence from wills and inventories suggests that there was a considerable increase among not only the gentry but also the yeomen and the urban middle classes towards the end of the sixteenth century. The proportion of Worcester lay inventories mentioning books seems to have increased from about 4 per cent in the period 1550–89 to 16 per cent in the 1590s and first decades of the seventeenth century. Moreover, the stock of books maintained in Shrewsbury by the Shropshire-born printer Roger Ward indicates that there was a considerable market for books on the Welsh border. When his goods were valued in 1585 his bookshop was found to contain nearly

2500 volumes. The contents were predominantly religious and included hundreds of prayer books, catechisms and psalters together with some 13 Bibles or parts of the Bible as well as commentaries on the Scriptures by Calvin and Theodore Beza. There was a large stock, too, of popular devotional works and over 200 books of sermons. Of the secular works in stock, the grammars and works by classical writers were no doubt aimed primarily at the pupils of Shrewsbury school. The range of the other secular works, however, which included almanacs, historical romances, books on the law, medicine, history, music and cookery, reflects the broadening and diversification of mental interests which took place in the Elizabethan period for reasons mainly independent of the Reformation and which added a new dimension to provincial culture.

As far as educational facilities were concerned, the impact of the Reformation made itself felt in several ways. The destructive effects of the dissolution of the religious houses in 1539 and the chantries in 1548 were offset to a considerable extent by the improvements and new foundations effected by the government. Indeed, it seems likely that the dissolutions have been overestimated as a force for good or bad in the history of education which, before and after the Reformation, continued to be largely provided in free schools endowed by private benefactors or by professional masters for a fee.

The determination on the part of the reformers and later the puritans to improve the level of religious knowledge among both clergy and laity contributed to the growth of interest in education which took place in the course of the sixteenth century. Education was one of the chief beneficiaries of the many hundreds of bequests and deeds of gift in the second half of the century which were directed to charitable purposes rather than to the church as in the pre-Reformation period. The wills of London merchants who established schools in the provinces and set up scholarship funds showed a determination to help able and aspiring children, however poor, to gain instruction not only in reading, writing and grammar but also in the holy gospel. Nor was this philanthropy confined to rich merchants. A yeoman of Wednesbury in Staffordshire made provision in his will in 1603 for a schoolmaster to give free tuition to ten poor children from families in Wednesbury. By the Elizabethan period evidence from diocesan records suggests that educational facilities were readily accessible in many parts of the country. Margaret Spufford has shown that Cambridgeshire was well provided with schools, while in the area of the west midlands and borders diocesan records indicate that there were, at a *minimum,* schoolmasters in some 44 towns or villages in Cheshire and some 60 towns or villages in the diocese of Hereford in the Elizabethan period. Few petty schoolmasters were licensed and recorded in the diocesan papers and the numbers of schoolmasters were also swollen by individuals such as Jacob Naishe, a yeoman of Henbury, Gloucestershire, who recorded in his will in 1574 the debts that were owing to him from their parents for teaching three boys to read and write, and Mrs Reade of Campden in Gloucestershire to whom Thomas Congreve, a Staffordshire gentleman, sent his youngest daughter Margaret, aged eleven, to read and sew in 1605.

The growth of interest in education is further illustrated by the large number of bequests in wills of the second half of the sixteenth century for the education of the testators' children. These bear witness to the increasing concern on the part of yeomen and the urban "bourgeoisie" that their children should receive an adequate education. How far down the social scale this concern extended is difficult to assess. It seems improbable, as Margaret Spufford has argued in her study of schooling in Cambridgeshire, that labourers and small farmers would have been able to release their sons from work in the fields for educational purposes. Nevertheless, the provision made by educational benefactors of the Elizabethan period for the poor must have spread educational opportunities more widely, particularly in the towns.

While provincial culture at all levels at the end of the sixteenth century remained predominantly religious, its emphasis had shifted from the ritualised, visual effects of the pre-Reformation period to the printed word. The development of the printing press played an important part in this transition but, underlying it, there was the emphasis of the Reformation on the need for direct study of the Bible. This transition involved a change in the whole way of life of many local communities for it entailed the abolition not only of religious rituals but also of many civic ceremonies. Its positive contribution to provincial culture lay in the stimulus it gave to the development of an informed approach to religion which made possible the emergence by the 1640s of a whole range of different religious viewpoints. The impact of the change can be traced among educated laymen not only from the gentry but also from the yeomen and middle classes in the towns whose wills bear witness to the spread of bookownership, particularly of the Bible, and the growth of interest in education. The consequences of this change for popular culture were perhaps even more significant—by giving humble men and women access to the text of the Scriptures, the Reformation laid the ground for the development at a popular level too of a more articulate approach to religion and the concept of religion as a pattern of beliefs rather than a series of ritual observances.

Richard G. Cole

PAMPHLET PROPAGANDA IN THE REFORMATION

The development of the printing press just a few decades before the beginning of Luther's revolt provided propagandists with a new, powerful weapon. Richard G. Cole, professor of history at Luther College, Decorah, Iowa, has published several articles on the pamphlet literature of the Reformation, and has analyzed the pamphleteer's role in shaping popular opinion.

S CHOLARS toward the end of the fifteenth century enjoyed a perfected printing technology and its products, beautiful folio *Bibles,* dictionaries, classical and medieval works, and a variety of secular publications. The sixteenth-century pamphlet represents a marked shift in the use of the printing press, a shift most noticeable in German areas and one coinciding with Reformation. The brief, blunt, and vulgar reformation tract intended for a wide and unlearned if not confused audience became a major tool of those who sought change in the religious loyalties of large numbers of people.

There is some evidence to illustrate the contention that those holding firmly to Catholicism ignored the propagandistic po-

From Richard G. Cole, "The Reformation in Print: German Pamphlets and Propaganda," *Archive for Reformation History,* vol. 66 (1975), pp. 93-102. Reprinted by permission of the Gütersloher Verlagshaus Gerd Mohn.

tential of the printing press. It is possible that Catholic theologians and statesmen who were long accustomed to power and authority felt little need to experiment with radically new methods of mass communication. Catholic reluctance was reinforced by tactile medieval habits of oral, visual, and ceremonial methods of communication. As late as 1590, for example, handwritten liturgical books were still in demand for use in Catholic churches and there were a number of ecclesiastics who would not pray from a printed book. For Protestants the power of the spoken word in and out of the pulpit or in disputation was important; yet, the print dimension appears to be a primary if not generic aspect of the Reformation process.

The influence of Reformation events on communication forms has not received adequate attention. Fortunately for students of sixteenth-century pamphlet literature, a large and representative sample collected by the nineteenth century man of letters, Gustav Freytag, is extant and has been superbly catalogued by Paul Hohenemser for the City and University Library in Frankfurt am Main. Hohenemser was familiar with the collecting methods of Gustav Freytag and realized that Freytag's collection is a reasonable sample of small book and pamphlet production. When viewed against what is commonly known about sixteenth-century printing, the Freytag Collection offers an excellent opportunity to speculate from a base of solid data about the patterns of print especially during the early decades of the sixteenth century.

This writer used an electronic computer to tabulate and sort a large body of factual data gleaned from Hohenemser's catalog, i.e., author, title, printer, place of origin, year of publication, format, number of pages and one of twenty-two category classifications ranging from cook books to works on astrology and polemical tracts. For a variety of reasons, many pamphlets were anonymous, had no date, or printer; these were coded and included in the analysis. The computer program digested eight-hundred and ninety-four authors, three-hundred and ninety-one printers, and one-hundred and twenty-five places of publication, and compared each of the latter items with each of the twenty-two categories. Then, the computer cross-tabulated printer against year, place against year and several more items pertaining to format. Data indicating printer, place, format, size, number of editions by year are impossible to handle in any meaningful way without electronic sorting and tabulation.

The computerized results support the contention that Protestants expressed themselves typographically in polemical matters to a significantly higher degree than Catholics. The prolific authors of polemical and related categories of Satire, Folk Songs and Verse comprise a list analogous to a hagiography of the entire sixteenth-century Reformation movement: Melachthon, Carlstadt, Rhegius, Zwingli, Linck, Osiander, Flacius, Oecolampadius, Bugenhagen, Kettenbach, and Brenz. As expected, Luther ranked first among the pamphleteers with eleven and one-half percent of the sixteenth-century portion of the Freytag sample of over three-thousand pamphlets. On the Catholic side there is no equivalent in the polemical area. Only Johann Cochlaeus, Johann Eck, the author-printer Thomas Murner, Hieronymous Emser and a few others emerge as Catholic protagonists. Recently, Rudolf Hirsch asserted that Catholic pamphlets, for example those of Cochlaeus, were difficult to sell because of their heavy style, great length and tendency to read like scholastic disputations. Often cited for the lack of Catholic response to Lutheran polemics are complex local ordinances designed to protect local printers or the Lutheran position.

One curious result occurring in the tabulation of the raw number of editions produced by those interested in Reformation was that next to Luther in pamphlet authorship was the relatively unknown reformer, Johann Eberlin von Günzburg. Eberlin, who early in the Reformation left his order of Franciscan Observants, produced in a short time a large number of polemical and Reformation pamphlets. In 1521 he published his most famous work, the *15 Bundesgenossen,* a series of pamphlets ranging from eight to thirty-two pages. Three editions of the *15 Bundesgenossen* appeared in 1521, one in Basel, one in Augsburg, and one in Speyer. Eberlin pointed out the need for religious reformation and at the same time called for Utopian socio-economic and political change. Whatever importance Eberlin may have had as an evangelistic reformer in south Germany, he is of interest here primarily for his clear conception of the polemical value of the print dimension. In his first pamphlet of 1521, Eberlin writes about the "new and useful art of bookprinting" which allows people "to know good writing, useful saying, evangelical doctrine, truth and wisdom." On numerous occasions Eberlin tells his readers that he considers himself a schoolmaster teaching a wide audience through his printed tracts. Aware of the many dangers inherent in the publication of inexpensive and quickly written materials, Eberlin insisted his books be printed by printers of integrity who carefully proofread and who used fine type and quality paper.

The use of pamphlets by dozens of reformers in some ways created a Reformation in print. There were new authorities to cite, new tools for education, new processes involved, all heightened by the authority of the printed word. As Eberlin mentioned to his readers, if you have questions on the sacraments, read a pamphlet by Dr. Martin Luther.

Before 1518 there was little pamphlet activity. In the year 1524 there was a thousand percent increase in the production of pamphlet editions, using 1517 as the base year. The great majority of important pamphlet centers (Basel, Nürnberg, Erfurt, Augsburg, Strassburg, Wittenberg, and Zwickau) had their highest pamphlet production in all categories in either 1523 or 1524. *Anno 1524,* "the year of the flood" according to Rhegius, was not a time of much printing activity in cities under strong Catholic in-

fluence, e.g., Leipzig, Tübingen and Landshut. In Landshut there was a strong printing establishment operated by Johann Weyssenburger. Prior to 1524, Weyssenburger had printed copies of the Papal Bull against Luther, and reprinted several pamphlets by Johann Eck and Johann Eckhard. In the "year of the flood" of the Reformation tracts, Weyssenburger printed only astrological predications and some of Eck's books in Latin. In Tübingen the practitioner of the black art, Ulrich Morhart, produced a number of pamphlets by Eck, Cochlaeus, Schatzgeyer, Faber, and Dietenberger. Morhart published Catholic works reluctantly since he had covert Lutheran sympathies. In Leipzig, Duke George discouraged further pamphlet activity after a flurry in 1519 and 1520. In all of the forty-three German cities producing pamphlets in the 1520's, Leipzig ranks near the bottom in pamphlet production. Even the great printing center and commercial city of Nürnberg was not an especially attractive place for any but the more moderate of printers.

Overall, the years 1521–1525 rank highest in pamphlet production for the whole of the sixteenth century with a sharp drop after 1525 and then a significant increase beginning in the 1530's, peaking in 1546 and remaining high until 1555. These trends in the Freytag Collection are almost identical to what is generally known about patterns of printing in the sixteenth century. This publication pattern suggests that periods of tension stimulated strong responses in the book market.

Individual authors and their work are only half of the story of the typographic revolution. It is clear that Reformation printers formed an important part of the rapidly growing pool of typographic men and women who played a significant role in shaping the process of Reformation. Printers were often educated, skilled and versatile individuals. Unfortunately, relatively little is known of biographical details, motivations, successes or failures of most printers. The career of the wealthy *Bible* printer and mayor of Wittenberg, Hans Lufft, is probably an exception. Some printers were authors in their own right. Eberlin's printer in Basel, Pamphilus Gengenbach was one of the first to write poetry in the vernacular and he wrote several pamphlets ranging from a critique of the *Bundschuh* (1514) to a tract (1523) published shortly before he died on the high cost of funerals. Gengenbach's most successful work, *Der Ewangelisch Burger* (1522) is a strong statement of Lutheran theology and appeals to townsmen to accept the Lutheran faith. Gengenbach's literary style is pedantic and lacks the appeal of works by Eberlin, Rhegius and Luther but Gengenbach does adhere to the Protestant virtue of brevity averaging sixteen pages per tract.

If the need arose, printers frequently added prefaces to works they accepted for publication. The anonymous printer of one of the first printed versions of the Leipzig Debate (Melchior Lotter d. A.?) set forth the reasons why the debate should be published as accurately and fairly as possible even though he was sensitive to the fact that he would be criticized for publishing the work. The printer commented that the debate seemed to be a "chaotic sea of words," i.e., it did not make much sense; he hoped the reader would judge for himself. This particular printer denoted a mixing of medias; the medieval oral disputation did not lend itself to the medium of the printed pamphlet. Karlstadt's famous book shuffle at Leipzig and Eck's caustic statements about Karlstadt's poor memory may indicate not so much the mental superiority of Eck and the bumbling mediocrity of Karlstadt but rather a methodological gap, one medieval and oral and one modern and typographic. Karlstadt's love of printed books elevated to the point that he invited the printer Nickel Schirlentz to live and work in his house.

In the 1520's about twenty printers dominated the production of polemical pamphlets. . . . Of all these printers only Johann Grüninger in Strassburg was Catholic, the remainder were all Lutheran in sympathy. Using the year 1523 as a sample year, one notes that there were seven working printers in Wittenberg, six of them emerge as prolific pamphlet printers. In Augsburg there are nine active printers in 1523; four of them are mentioned above and four others are clearly identified with Reformation and are included in the Freytag Collection. In contrast, Nürnberg had five active printers in 1523, most of whom dared not use their name or device on a pamphlet. In the years from 1523 to 1529, there are eighty more printers represented in the Freytag sample. These too numerous to mention printers published from one to six editions in subject categories dominated by Reformation authors. These publications stemmed from about thirty towns and cities not mentioned above. Unfortunately, forty-five percent of the sixteenth century pamphlets in the collection under study have not been pinpointed as to author, place of origin or printer.

The smallness and general insignificance of both some of the printers and places of publication offer a marked contrast to publishers of conventional works or to publishers of the incunabula who worked in the larger commercial, episcopal, and Imperial Cities. Wide printing dispersal indicates a changing market pattern for books. It was cheaper to print tracts nearer to the location where they were sold. Packing and shipment of printed materials often proved to be expensive. Decentralized printing coupled with the fact that pamphlet printers strongly identified with Reformation created a web of print that became inexorably connected with the fate of Protestantism.

To some extent printers and their colporteurs were in business for profit and they exploited a favorable market. As Aleander, the Papal nuncio wrote to Leo X (Feb. 8, 1521) that vernacular Lutheran propaganda was "so popular that book printers will not sell anything but Lutheran writing." Aleander's report while partly accurate is misleading *vis-à-vis* the economic motives of printers. Although profit was necessary in the highly competitive business of printing, many printers had strong ideological commitments. Ernst Schwiebert points out in his Valparaiso lectures that when a shortage of trained clergy arose in the early years of the Reformation and *Notprediger* had to be called to service, printers became emergency preachers at a ratio of ten to one when compared with merchants, stonemasons, or clothiers. The ratio of printers becoming preachers was four to one when compared with schoolmasters.

The typographic men and women of the Reformation were seeking with the pamphlet medium to overcome what Lucien Febvre calls *une force d'inertie* among the literate public. Pamphleteers strongly believed in their new medium and estimated the impact of their work to be great. Thus, many authors were outspoken over the possibility of misinterpretations arising from printer's errors or from their own stylistic deficiencies. Karlstadt, for example, found it difficult to write without becoming abusively personal which "might scandalize my brother and bring me into Judgment." Urbanus Rhegius certainly agreed with Karlstadt's candor. Rhegius writes of Karlstadt: "You write with the cunningness of a wounded wolf." In the matter of inaccurate printing Karlstadt complained that whole columns were discarded and sentences muddled. Luther and Eberlin voiced similar complaints. At times, materials were published that could be read in a fashion entirely opposite of the original intention. A case in point is a pamphlet by Urbanus Rhegius who was essentially conservative and cautious and who abhorred violence of any type. Yet in a printed version of his 1522 sermon on the "Reorganization of the Church" we read: "The *Scriptures* tell us what we should or should not do." The text is cited as Deuteronomy 12; no further explanation of Deuteronomy follows. If the reader looked up the passage cited by Rhegius or scanned his memory, he would note the following verbs in the first three verses. You shall "destroy, tear down, dash, burn, and hew down the temples of false gods." Those who knew Rhegius or his approach to Reformation would not misinterpret; the unlearned or semi-literate who according to Erasmus were legion could easily become confused.

One aspect of assessing the impact of pamphlets which is essentially out of the scope of this paper is the emblematic significance of the illustrated title pages. Woodcut illustrations which were particularly rich and creative in the 1520's offered clues to prospective buyers concerning the contents of the booklet. It may be worth noting that the Florentine border on Rhegius's pamphlet mentioned above is incredibly serene. Quite in contrast is a letter of Thomas Müntzer published in 1525. The border on the title page depicts a peasant with a bow and arrow aimed dead center at an unaware and unsuspecting nobleman carrying a firearm.

Many conclusions have been drawn in the last two centuries relative to the value, significance and meaning of the Reformation pamphlet. Typical is August Baur's statement that pamphlets were significant penetration vehicles for Protestant thought into German cultural life in the Reformation epoch. Few scholars would dispute Baur's statement even though it is limited in scope. The pamphlet explosion of the 1520's should be viewed as a typographic revolution coinciding with the early dynamic years of Reformation. Printing as a technology had matured in western Europe and the pamphlet is in many respects an example of a ripe technology. The octavo and quarto formats represent the inevitable miniaturization accompanying technological maturity. The mass production of printed pages, the creation of a wide market, and the apparent increase in literacy created a new world of small books, a Reformation in print.

Many Protestants realized the delicate interplay of printed communication and controversy; indeed, the dynamic and successful leadership of the Reformation had a special creative and psychological affinity for the exploitation of the pamphlet genre. Some important differences between Reformers and leaders of the establishment can be defined in terms of attitudes toward media. It is almost axiomatic that book and press were crucial tools in reordering values in the sixteenth century.

Natalie Zemon Davis

CITY WOMEN AND THE REFORMATION

Natalie Davis, professor of history at Princeton University, has established herself as a foremost authority on the Reformation. Her keen social analyses of the French Reformation have won international recognition, including the *Ordre des Palmes académiques* and the presidency of both the American Society for Reformation Research and the Society for French Historical Studies. Her book, *Society and Culture in Early Modern France,* from which the following selection is taken, received the Berkshire Conference Prize for Historical Scholarship.

APART FROM the religious, almost all adult urban women in the first half of the sixteenth century were married or had once been so. The daughter of a rich merchant, lawyer, or financial officer might find herself betrothed in her late teens. Most women waited until their early twenties, when a dowry could be pieced together from the family or one's wages or extracted from a generous master or mistress.

And then the babies began and kept appearing every two or three years. The wealthy woman, with her full pantry and her country refuge in times of plague, might well raise six or seven children to adulthood. The artisan's wife might bury nearly as many as she bore, while the poor woman was lucky to have even one live through the perils of a sixteenth-century childhood. Then, if she herself had managed to survive the first rounds of childbearing and live into her thirties, she might well find that her husband had not. Remarriage was common, of course, and until certain restrictive edicts of the French king in the 1560's a widow could contract it quite freely. If she then survived her husband into her forties, chances are she would remain a widow. At this stage of life, women outnumbered and outlived men, and

even the widow sought after for her wealth might prefer independence to the relative tutelage of marriage.

With the death rate so high, the cities of sixteenth-century France depended heavily on immigration for their increasing populations. Here, however, we find an interesting difference between the sexes: men made up a much larger percentage of the young immigrants to the cities. The male immigrants contributed to every level of the vocational hierarchy—from notaries, judges, and merchants to craftsmen and unskilled day laborers. And although most of the men came from nearby provinces, some were also drawn from faraway cities and from regions outside the kingdom of France. The female immigrants, on the other hand, clustered near the bottom of the social ladder and came mostly from villages and hamlets in surrounding provinces to seek domestic service in the city.

Almost all the women took part in one way or another in the economic life of the city. The picture drawn in Renaissance courtesy books and suggested by the quotation from Robert Mandrou—that of women remaining privily in their homes—is rather far from the facts revealed by judicial records and private contracts. The wife of

Reprinted from Natalie Zemon Davis, *Society and Culture in Early Modern France* (Stanford University Press, Stanford, 1975), pp. 69-85, 86-94. Reprinted by permission of the Stanford University Press.

the wealthy lawyer, royal officer, or prosperous merchant supervised the productive activities of a large household but might also rent out and sell rural and urban properties in her own name, in her husband's name, or as a widow. The wives of tradesmen and master craftsmen had some part in running the shops, not just when they were widowed but also while their husbands were alive: a wife might discipline apprentices (who sometimes resented being beaten by a woman's hand), might help the journeymen at the large looms, might retail meats while her husband and his workers slaughtered cattle, might borrow money with her husband for printing ventures, and so on.

In addition, a significant proportion of women in artisanal families and among the *menu peuple* had employ on their own. They worked especially in the textile, clothing, leather, and provisioning trades, although we can also find girls apprenticed to pinmakers and gilders. They sold fish and tripe; they ran inns and taverns. They were painters and, of course, midwives. In Paris they made linen; in Lyon they prepared silk. They made shoes and gloves, belts and collars. . . .

Finally, there were the various semiskilled or unskilled jobs done by women. Domestic service involved a surprisingly high number of girls and women. Even a modest artisanal family was likely to have a wretchedly paid serving girl, perhaps acquired from within the walls of one of the orphan-hospitals recently set up in many urban centers. There was service in the bathhouses, which sometimes slid into prostitution. Every city had its *filles de joie*, whom the town council tried to restrict to certain streets and to stop from brazenly soliciting clients right in front of the parish church. And there was heavy work, such as ferrying people across the Saône and other rivers, the boatwomen trying to argue up their fares as they rowed. If all else failed, a woman could dig ditches and carry things at the municipal construction sites. For this last, she worked shoulder to shoulder with unskilled male day workers, being paid about one-half or two-thirds as much as they for her pains.

This economic activity of women among the *menu peuple* may explain in part the funny nicknames that some of them had. Most French women in the sixteenth century kept their maiden names all their lives: when necessary, the phrase "wife of" or "widow of" so-and-so was tacked on. Certain women, however, had sobriquets: *la Capitaine des vaches* (the Captain of the cows) and *la reine d'Hongrie* (the queen of Hungary) were nicknames given to two women who headed households in Lyon; *la Catelle* was a schoolmistress in Paris; *la Varenne*, a midwife in Le Mans; and *la Grosse Marguerite*, a peddler of Orléans. Such names were also attached to very old women. But in all cases, we can assume not only that these women were a little eccentric but also that these names were bestowed on them in the course of public life—in the street, in the marketplace, or in the tavern.

The public life of urban women did not, however, extend to the civic assembly or council chamber. Women who were heads of households do appear on tax lists and even on militia rolls and were expected to supply money or men as the city government required. But that was the extent of political participation for the *citoyenne*. Male artisans and traders also had little say in these oligarchical city governments, but at least the more prosperous among them might have hoped to influence town councillors through their positions as guild representatives. The guild life of women, however, was limited and already weaker than it had been in the later Middle Ages. In short, the political activity of women on all levels of urban society was indirect or informal only. The wives of royal officers or town councillors might have hoped to influence powerful men at their dining tables. The wives of poor and powerless journeymen and day laborers, when their tables were bare because the city fathers had failed to provide the town with grain, might have tried to change things by joining with their husbands and children in a well-timed grain riot.

What of the literacy of urban women in the century after the introduction of printing to Europe? In the families of the urban elite the women had at least a vernacular education—usually at the hands of private tutors—in French, perhaps in Italian, in music, and in arithmetic. A Latin education among nonnoble city women was rare enough that it was remarked—"learned beyond her sex," the saying went—and a girl like Louise Sarrasin of Lyon, whose physician-father had started her in Hebrew, Greek, and Latin by the time she was eight, was considered a wondrous prodigy. It was women from these wealthy families of bankers and jurists who organized the important literary salons in Paris, Lyon, Poitiers, and elsewhere.

Once outside these restricted social circles, however, there was a dramatic drop in the level of education and of mere literacy among city women. An examination of contracts involving some 1,200 people in Lyon in the 1560's and 1570's to see whether those people could simply sign their names reveals that, of the women, only 28 percent could sign their names. These were almost all from the elite families of well-off merchants and publishers, plus a few wives of surgeons and goldsmiths. All the other women in the group—the wives of mercers, of artisans in skilled trades, and even of a few notaries—could not sign. This is in contrast to their husbands and to male artisans generally, whose ability to sign ranged from high among groups like printers, surgeons, and goldsmiths, to moderate among men in the leather and textile trades, to low—although still well above zero—among men in the food and construction trades. Thus, in the populous middle rank of urban society, although both male and female literacy may have risen from the mid-fifteenth century under the impact of economic growth and the invention of printing, the literacy of the men increased much more than that of the women. Tradesmen might have done business with written accounts; tradeswomen more often had to use finger reckoning, the abacus, or counting stones. Only at the bottom of the social hierarchy, among the unskilled workers and urban gardeners, were men and women alike. As with peasants,

there were few of either sex who were literate.

And where would women of artisanal families learn to read and write if their fathers and husbands did not teach them? Nunnery schools received only a small number of lay girls, and these only from fine families. The municipal colleges set up in the first half of the sixteenth century in Toulouse, Nîmes, and Lyon were for boys only; so were most of the little vernacular schools that mushroomed in even quite modest city neighborhoods during these years. To be sure, a few schoolmistresses were licensed in Paris, and there were always some Parisian schoolmasters being chided for illegally receiving girls along with their boy pupils. But in Lyon, where I have found only five female teachers from the 1490's to the 1560's, I have come upon 87 schoolmasters for the same decades.

Thus, in the first half of the sixteenth century, the wealthy and well-born woman was being encouraged to read and study by the availability to her of printed books; by the strengthening of the image of the learned lady, as the writings of Christine de Pisan and Marguerite de Navarre appeared in print; and by the attitude of some fathers, who took seriously the modest educational programs for women being urged by Christian humanists like Erasmus and Juan Luis Vives. Reading and writing for women of the *menu peuple* was more likely to be ridiculous, a subject for farce.

All this shows how extraordinary was the achievement of Louise Labé, the one lowborn female poet of sixteenth-century France. From a family of Lyon ropemakers, barber-surgeons, and butchers, in which some of the women were literate and some (including her own stepmother) were not, Louise was beckoned to poetry and publication by her talent and by profane love. Her message to women in 1555 was "to lift their minds a little above their distaffs and spindles . . . to apply themselves to science and learning . . . and to let the world know that if we are not made to command, we must not for that be disdained as companions, both in domestic and public affairs, of those who govern and are obeyed."

The message of Calvinist reformers to women also concerned reading and patterns of companionship. But before we turn to it, let us see what can be said about the Catholic religious activity of city women on the eve of the French Reformation.

In regard to the sacramental life of the church, the women behaved very much like their husbands. The prominent families, in which the husband was on the parish building committee, attended mass and confession with some regularity. The wealthiest of them also had private chapels in their country homes. Among the rest of the population attendance was infrequent, and it was by no means certain that all the parishioners would even get out once a year to do their Easter duty of confession and communion. (The clergy itself was partly to blame for this. Those big city parishes were doubling and even tripling in size in these decades, and yet the French Church took virtually no steps to increase accordingly its personnel in charge of pastoral functions or even to guarantee confessors who could understand the language and dialect of the parishioners.) Baptism was taken more seriously, however, as were marriage and extreme unction. Every two or three years the husband appeared before the *curé* with the new baby, bringing with him one or two godfathers and up to five godmothers. The wife was most likely at home, waiting till she was ready to get up for her "churching," or purification after childbirth (the *relevailles)*. Moreover, the wills of both men and women show an anxious preoccupation with the ceremonial processions at their funerals and masses to be said for the future repose of their souls. A chambermaid or male weaver might invest many months' salary in such arrangements.

In regard to the organizational and social aspects of Catholic piety on the eve of the Reformation, however, the woman's position was somewhat different from the man's. On the one hand, female religious life was less well organized than male religious life; on the other, the occasions in which urban women participated jointly

with men in organized lay piety were not as frequent as they might have been.

To be sure, parish processions led by the priests on Corpus Christi and at other times included men, women, and children, and so did the general processions of the town to seek God's help in warding off famine or other disasters. But the heart of lay religious activity in France in the early sixteenth century was in the lay confraternities organized around crafts or around some devotional interests. Here laymen could support common masses, have their own banquets (whose excesses the clergy deplored), and mount processions on their own saints' days—with "blessed bread," music, costumes, and plays. City women were members of confraternities in much smaller numbers than men at this period. For instance, out of 37 confraternities at Rouen in the first half of the sixteenth century, only six mention female members, and these in small proportion. Women were formally excluded from the important Confraternity of the Passion at Paris, and some confraternities in other cities had similar provisions. Young unmarried men were often organized into confraternities under the patronage of Saint Nicholas; young unmarried women prayed to Saint Catherine, but religious organizations of female youth are hard to find.

Even the convents lacked vitality as centers of organization at this time. Fewer in number than the male religious houses in France and drawing exclusively on noble or wealthy urban families for their membership, the convents were being further isolated by the "reform" movements of the early sixteenth century. Pushed back into arid enclosure, the nuns were cut off not only from illicit love affairs but also from rich contact with the women in the neighborhoods in which they lived. Nor in France during the first part of the sixteenth century do we hear of any new female experiments with communal living, work, and spiritual perfection like the late medieval Beguinages or the imaginative Ursuline community just then being created in an Italian city.

Thus, before the Reformation the relation of Catholic lay women to their saints was ordinarily private or informally organized. The most important occasions for invoking the saints were during pregnancy and especially during childbirth. Then, before her female neighbors and her midwife, the parturient woman called upon the Virgin—or, more likely, upon Saint Margaret, patron of pregnant women—that God might comfort her peril and pain and that her child might issue forth alive.

Into this picture of city women separated from their parish clergy and from male religious organizations, one new element was to enter, even before the Reformation. Women who could read or who were part of circles where reading was done aloud were being prompted by vernacular devotional literature and the Bible to speculate on theology. "Why, they're half theologians," said the Franciscan preachers contemptuously. They own Bibles the way they own love stories and romances. They get carried away by questions on transubstantiation, and they go "running around from . . . one [male] religious house to another, seeking advice and making much ado about nothing." What the good brothers expected from city women was not silly reasoning but the tears and repentance that would properly follow a Lenten sermon replete with all the rhetorical devices and dramatic gestures of which the Franciscans were masters.

Even a man who was more sympathetic than the Franciscans to lettered females had his reservations about how far their learning should take them. A male poet praised the noble dame Gabrielle de Bourbon in the 1520's for reading vernacular books on moral and doctrinal questions and for composing little treatises to the honor of God and the Virgin Mary. But she knew her limits, for "women must not apply their minds to curious questions of theology and the secret matters of divinity, the knowledge of which belongs to prelates, rectors and doctors."

The Christian humanist Erasmus was one of the few men of his time who sensed the depths of resentment accumulating in women whose efforts to think about doctrine were not taken seriously by the clergy. In one of his *Colloquies,* a lady learned in Latin and Greek is being twitted by an asinine abbot (the phrase is Erasmus'). She finally bursts out, "If you keep on as you've begun, geese may do the preaching sooner than put up with you tongue-tied pastors. The world's a stage that's topsy-turvy now, as you see. Every man must play his part—or exit."

The world was indeed topsy-turvy. The Catholic Church, which Erasmus had tried to reform from within, was being split by Protestants who believed that man was saved by faith in Christ alone and that human work had nothing to do with it, who were changing the sacramental system all around and overthrowing the order of the priesthood. Among this welter of new ideas, let us focus here on the new image of the Christian woman as presented in Calvinist popular literature.

We can find her in a little play dated around 1550. The heroine is not a learned lady but a pure and simple woman who knows her Bible. The villain is not a teasing, harmless abbot but a lecherous and stupid village priest. He begins by likening her achievements to those of craftsmen who were meddling with Scripture, and then goes on: "Why, you'll even see a woman / Knock over your arguments / With her responses on the Gospel." And in the play she does, quoting Scripture to oppose the adoration of Mary and the saints and to oppose the power of the popes. The priest can only quote from glosses, call her names, and threaten to burn her.

Wherever one looks in the Protestant propaganda of the 1540's to the 1560's, the Christian woman is identified by her relation to Scripture. Her sexual purity and control are demonstrated by her interest in the Bible, and her right to read the New Testament in the vernacular is defended against those who would forbid it to her, as to such other unlearned persons as merchants and artisans. The author of the pamphlet *The Way to Arrive at the Knowledge of God* put the matter sharply enough: "You say that women who want to read the Bible are just libertines? I say you call them lewd merely because they won't consent to your seduction. You say it's permitted to women to read Boccaccio's *Flamette* or Ovid's *Art of Love* ... which teach them to be adulterers, and yet you'll send a woman who's reading a Bible to the flames. You say it's enough for a woman's salvation for her to do her housework, sew and spin? ... Of what use then are Christ's promises to her? You'll put spiders in Paradise, for they know how to spin very well."

The message was even put to music during the First Religious War in the 1560's. The Huguenot queen of Navarre sings:

> Those who say it's not for women
> To look at Holy Writ
> Are evil men and infamous
> Seducers and antichrist.
> Alas, my ladies.
> Your poor souls
> Let them not be governed
> By such great devils.

And in reality as well as in popular literature Protestant women were freeing their souls from the rule of priests and doctors of theology. Noble churchmen were horrified at the intemperance with which Protestant females abused them as godless men. The pages of Jean Crespin's widely read *Book of the Martyrs,* based on the real adventures of Protestant heretics, record the story of one Marie Becaudelle, a servant of La Rochelle who learns of the Gospel from her master and argues publicly with a Franciscan, showing him from Scripture that he does not preach according to the Word of God. A bookseller's wife disputes doctrine in a prison cell with the bishop of Paris and with doctors of theology. An honest widow of Tours talks to priests and monks with the witness of Scripture: "I'm a sinner, but I don't need candles to ask God to pardon my faults. You're the ones who walk in darkness." The learned theologians did not know what to make of such monstrous women, who went against nature.

To this challenge to the exclusion of women, the Catholic theologians in mid-century responded not by accommodating but by digging in their heels. It wasn't safe, said an important Jesuit preacher, to leave the Bible to the discretion of "what's turning around in a woman's brain." "To learn essential doctrine," echoed another cleric, "there is no need for women or artisans to take time out from their work and read the Old and New Testament in the vernacular. Then they'll want to dispute about it and give their opinion ... and they can't help falling into error. Women must be silent in Church, as Saint Paul says." Interestingly enough, when a Catholic vernacular Bible was finally allowed to circulate in France at the end of the sixteenth century, it did not play an important role in the conversion or devotional life of Catholic leaders like Barbe Acarie and Saint Jeanne Frances de Chantal.

Thus, into a pre-Reformation situation in which urban women were estranged from priests or in tension with them over the matter of their theological curiosity, the Protestant movement offered a new option: relations with the priestly order could be broken, and women, like their husbands (indeed *with* their husbands), could be engaged in the pure and serious enterprise of reading and talking about Scripture. The message being broadcast to male artisans and lesser merchants was similar but less momentous. In the first place, the men were more likely already to be literate; and anyway, the only natural order the men were being asked to violate was the separation between the learned and unlearned. The women were *also* being called to a new relation with men. It is worth noting how different is this appeal to women from that which Max Weber considered most likely to win females over to a new religion. Rather than inciting to orgy and emotion, it was summoning to intellectual activity and self-control.

How was the appeal received? France never became a Protestant kingdom, of course, and even in cities where the movement was strong only one-third to one-half of the population might be ardent Calvinists. City men who became caught up in Protestantism ranged from wealthy bankers and professionals to poor journeymen, but they were generally from the more skilled and complex, the more literate, or the more novel trades and occupations. A printer, a goldsmith, or a barber-surgeon was more likely to disobey priests and doctors of theology than was a boatmaster, a butcher, or a baker.

What of the Calvinist women? As with the men, they did not come from the mass of poor unskilled people at the bottom of urban society, although a certain percentage of domestic servants did follow their masters and mistresses into the Reformed Church. The Protestant women belonged mostly to the families of craftsmen, merchants, and professional men, but they were by no means exclusively the literate women in these circles. For all the female martyrs who answered the Inquisitors by citing Scripture they had read, there were as many who could answer only by citing doctrines they had heard. It is also clear that in Lyon in the 1570's, more than a decade after the Reformed Church had been set up, a significant percentage of Reformed women still could not write their names. For this last group, then, the Protestant path was not a way to express their new literacy but a way finally to associate themselves with that surge of male literacy already described.

But there is more that we can say about city women who turned Protestant. A preliminary examination of women arrested for heresy or killed in Catholic uprisings in many parts of France, of women among the Protestant suspects in Toulouse in 1568-69, and of a very large sample of Protestant women in Lyon (about 750 women) yields three main observations. First, there is no clear evidence either that the wives mainly followed their husbands into the movement or that it worked the other way around. We can find women converted by their husbands who became more committed than their men; we can find wives who converted while their husbands remained "polluted in idolatry" and husbands who converted while their wives lagged behind. Second, the Protestant women seemed to include more than a random number of widows, of women with employ of their own—such as dressmakers, merchants, midwives, hotel-keepers, and the like—and of women with the curious nicknames associated with public and eccentric personalities. But finally, the Protestant movement in the sixteenth century did not pull in the small but significant group of genuinely learned women in the city—neither the patronesses of the literary salons nor the profane female poets. Louise Labé, who pleaded with women to lift their heads above their distaffs, always remained in the church that invoked the Virgin, although one of her aunts, a female barber, joined the Calvinists.

What do these observations suggest about the state of life of city women before their conversion to the new religion? They do not indicate a prior experience of mere futility and waste or restrictive little family worlds. Rather, Protestant religious commitment seems to have complemented in a new sphere the scope and independence that the women's lives had already had. Women already independent in the street and market now ventured into the male preserve of theology. And yet the literary woman, already admitted to the castle of learning, does not seem to have needed the Religion of the Book. A look at developments within the Reformed Church will indicate why this should have been so.

After 1562 the Reformed Church of France started to settle into its new institutional structures and the promise of Protestantism began to be realized for city women. Special catechism classes in French were set up for women, and in towns under Huguenot control efforts were made to encourage literacy, even among all the poor girls in the orphanages, not just the gifted few. In certain Reformed families the literate husbands finally began teaching their wives to read.

Some Protestant females, however, had more ambitious goals. The image of the new Christian woman with her Bible had beckoned them to more than catechism classes or reading the Scriptures with their husbands. Consider Marie Dentière. One-time abbess in Tournai, but expelled from her convent in the 1520's because of heresy, Dentière married a pastor and found her way to Geneva during its years of religious revolution. There, according to the report of a nun of the Poor Clare order, Marie got "mixed up with preaching," coming, for instance, to the convent to persuade the poor creatures to leave their miserable life. She also published two religious works, one of them an epistle on religious matters addressed to Princess Marguerite de Navarre. Here Dentière inserted a "Defense for Women" against calumnies, not only by Catholic adversaries but also by some of the Protestant faithful. The latter were saying that it was rash for women to publish works to each other on Scriptural matters. Dentière disagreed: "If God has done the grace to some poor women to reveal to them by His Holy Scriptures some good and holy thing, dare they not write about it, speak about it, and declare it, one to the other?. . . . Is it not foolishly done to hide the talent that God has given us?"

Dentière maintained the modest fiction that she was addressing herself only to other females. Later women did not. Some of the women prisoners in the French jails preached to "the great consolation" of both male and female listeners. [The] ex-Calvinist jurist Florimond de Raemond gave several examples, both from the Protestant conventicles and from the regular Reformed services as late as 1572, of women who while waiting for a preacher to arrive had gone up to pulpits and read from the Bible. One *théologienne* even took public issue with her pastor. Finally, in some of the Reformed Churches southwest of Paris—in areas where weavers and women had been early converts—a movement started to permit lay persons to prophesy. This would have allowed both women and unlearned men to get up in church and speak on holy things.

Jean Calvin, Théodore de Bèze, and other members of the Venerable Company of Pastors did not welcome these developments. The social thrust of the Reformation, as they saw it, was to overthrow the hierarchical priestly class and administer the church instead by well-trained pastors and sound male members of the Consistories. That was enough topsy-turvy for them. And like Catholic critics who had quoted Paul's dictum from I Corinthians that "women keep silence in the churches" against Protestants who were reading and talking about the Bible, now the Reformed pastors quoted it against Protestant women who wanted to preach publicly or have some special vocation in the church. Pierre Viret explained in 1560 that the elect were equal in that they were called to be Christian and faithful—man and woman, master and servant, free and serf. But the Gospel had not abolished within the church the rank and order of nature and of human society. God created and Christ confirmed that order. Even if a woman had greater spiritual gifts than had her husband, she could not speak in Christian assembly. Her task, said Pastor Viret, was merely to instruct her children in the faith when they were young; she might also be a schoolteacher to girls if she wished.

And when a female—even a member of the royal family, like Renée de France—tried to go beyond this and meddle in the affairs of the Consistory, the ministers could be very blunt. As a pastor wrote to Calvin about Renée, "She is turning everything upside-down in our ecclesiastical assembly. . . . . Our Consistory will be the laughing-stock of papists and Anabaptists. They'll say we're being ruled by women.

Women had been incited to disobey their priests: were they now going to be allowed to disobey their pastors? The pastors quelled them rather easily, and the noisy women subsided into silence or, in a few cases, returned to the Catholic Church. Interestingly enough, during the 1560's, when so many urban churches needed pastors, even a few men of artisanal background were scooped in as ministers of the Word. Consistories were dominated by wealthy merchants and professional men but usually included one or two prosperous master craftsmen. But the women, no matter how rich or well read, were just wives: together with men in a new relation to the Word—but unequal nevertheless.

It cannot be said that the French

Calvinist women expressed much bitterness about this role. Radical sects of the Anabaptist type did not form in France, as they did in the Netherlands or in Germany, where—in a less professional, less bookish, less hierarchical order—women were allowed to prophesy or speak in tongues along with men. Nor, apart from later witchcraft trials, did the French Reformation ever turn against troublemaking women with the fury of the Jacobins during the French Revolution, who guillotined the feminist leaders and denied women any political rights whatsoever, including the right even to witness political debate. What is notable about Calvinist women is not that they were subsequently discontented but that the Reformed solution gave a certain style to their activities on behalf of the Gospel. However enterprising the city women were in the cause of the New Jerusalem—and their activities ranged from marching to martyrdom—there were two things they did not do. No Calvinist woman showed (or was allowed to show) the organizational creativity of the great Catholic females of the Counter-Reformation—of an Angela Merici, for instance, who conceived and set up an extraordinary new order for nonenclosed women in Brescia in the 1530's. Nor did Reformed women outside the circles of the nobility publish as much as did Catholic women of the same social milieu. . . .

An examination of a few other areas of Protestant reform reveals the same pattern as in reading Scripture and preaching: city women revolted against priests and entered new religious relations that brought them together with men or likened them to men but left them unequal.

The new Calvinist liturgy, with its stress on the concerted fellowship of the congregation, used the vernacular—the language of women and the unlearned—and included Psalms sung jointly by men and women. Nothing shocked Catholic observers more than this. When they heard the music of male and female voices filtering from a house where a conventicle was assembled, all they could imagine were lewd activities with the candles extinguished. It was no better

when the Protestant movement came into the open. After the rich ceremony of the mass, performed by the clergy with due sanctity and grandeur, the Reformed service seemed, in the words of a Catholic in Paris in the 1560's, "without law, without order, without harmony." "The minister begins. Everybody follows—men, women, children, servants, chambermaids. . . . No one is on the same verse. . . .The fine-voiced maidens let loose their hums and trills . . . so the young men will be sure to listen. How wrong of Calvin to let women sing in Church."

To Protestant ears, it was very different. For laymen and laywomen in the service the common voice in praise of the Lord expressed the lack of distance between pastor and congregation. The Catholic priests had stolen the Psalms; now they had been returned. As for the participants in the conventicles, the songs gave them courage and affirmed their sense of purity over the hypocritical papists, who no sooner left the mass than they were singing love songs. The Protestant faithful were firmly in control of their sexual impulses, they believed, their dark and sober clothes a testimonial to their sincerity. And when the women and men sang together in the great armed street marches of the 1560's, the songs were a militant challenge to the hardened Catholics and an invitation to the wavering listeners to join the elect.

For the city women, there was even more novelty. They had had a role smaller than men's in the organized lay ceremonial life of the church, and the confraternities had involved them rather little. Previously, nuns had been the only women to sing the office. Now the confraternities and the convents would be abolished. The ceremonial was simplified and there was only one kind of group for worship, one in which men and women sang together. For Protestant tradesmen, many of whom were immigrants to the city, the new liturgical fellowship provided religious roots they had been unable to find in the inhospitable parishes. For Protestant women, who were not as likely to have been immigrants, the new liturgy provided roots in religious organizations with men.

But this leveling, this gathering together of men and women, had its limits. Singing in church did not lead women on to preaching or to participating in the Consistory and more than Bible-reading had. Furthermore, there was some effort by the pastors to order the congregations so as to reflect the social order. In Geneva, special seats were assigned to minimize the mingling of the sexes. And in some Reformed churches the sexes were separated when communion was taken: the men went up first to partake of the Holy Supper.

Psalms were added to the religious life of the Protestants and saints were taken away—from prayer, image, and invocation. Here the matter of sex was indifferent: Saint Damian departed as did Saint Margaret; Saint Nicholas departed as did Saint Catherine. Protestant men and women affirmed before the Inquisition that one must not call upon the Virgin, for, blessed though she was, she had no merit. And when the magistrates were slow to purify the churches of their idolatrous statues, zealous members of the *menu peuple* smashed the saints. Females were always included in these crowds. Indeed, like the armed march of the psalm-singers, the iconoclastic riot was a transfer of the joint political action of the grain riot into the religious sphere.

But the loss of the saints affected men and women unequally. Reformed prayer could no longer be addressed to a woman, whereas the masculine identity of the Father and Son was left intact. It may seem anachronistic to raise the matter of sexual identity in religious images during the Reformation, but it is not. Soon afterward, the Catholic poet Marie le Jars de Gournay, friend and editor of Montaigne, was to argue in her *Equality of the Sexes* that Jesus' incarnation as a male was no special honor to the male sex but a mere historical convenience; given the patriarchal malice of the Jews, a female savior would never have been accepted. But if one were going to emphasize the sex of Jesus, then it was all the more important to stress the perfection

of Mary and her role in the conception of our Lord. So, if the removal from Holy Mother Church cut off certain forms of religious affect for men, for women the consequences for their identities went even deeper. Now during their hours of childbirth—a "combat," Calvin described it, "a horrible torment"—they called no more on the Virgin and said no prayers to Saint Margaret. Rather, as Calvin advised, they groaned and sighed to the Lord and He received those groans as a sign of their obedience.

Obedience to the Lord was, of course, a matter for both men and women. But women had the additional charge of being obedient to their husbands. The Reformed position on marriage provides a final illustration of the pattern "together but unequal."

The Protestant critique of clerical celibacy involved first and foremost a downgrading of the concept that the male had a greater capacity than the female to discipline his sexual impulses. Since the time of the Greeks, physicians had been telling people that physiology made the female the more lustful, the more uncontrollable sex. As Doctor François Rabelais put it, there are many things a man can do, from work to wine, to control "the pricks of venery"; but a woman, with her hysteric animal (the womb) within, could rarely restrain herself from cuckolding her husband. Given these assumptions, clerical celibacy for the superior sex had been thought a real possibility whereas for the female it had appeared an exceptional achievement.

The Reformers' observation that continence was a rare gift of God and their admonition "Better to marry than to burn" were, then, primarily addressed to the numerous male clergy and less to the small fraction of female religious. Indeed, sermons on clerical marriage stressed how the groom would now be saved from fornication and hellfire but said little of the soul of the bride. It is surely significant, too, that male religious joined the Reformation movements in proportionately larger numbers than did female. The nuns were always the strong holdouts, even when they were promised dowries and pensions. Though some of them may have been afraid to try their chances on the marriage market, many simply preferred the separate celibate state and organization. When Marie Dentière tried to persuade the nuns of the Poor Clare order at Geneva to end their hypocritical lives and marry, as she had, the sisters spat at her.

The argument for clerical marriage, then, equalized men and women somewhat in regard to their appetites. It also raised the woman's status by affirming that she could be a worthy companion to a minister of God. The priest's concubine, chased from his house in ignominy by Catholic reformers and ridiculed as a harlot by Protestants, could now become the pastor's wife! A respectable girl from a good city family— likely, in the first generation, to be the daughter of a merchant or prosperous crafts-man—would be a helpful companion to her husband, keeping his busy household in order and his colleagues entertained. And she would raise her son to be a pastor and her daughter to be a pastor's wife.

Since marriage was now the only en-couraged state, the Reformers did what they could to make it more tolerable according to their lights. Friendship and companionship within marriage were stressed, as many historians have pointed out, although it is a mistake to think that this was unique to Protestant thought. Catholic humanist writ-ers valued these relations within marriage as well. In other ways, the Reformed position was more original. A single sexual standard would now be enforced rather than talked about; and the victorious Huguenot Con-sistories during the Wars of Religion chased out the prostitutes almost as quickly as they silenced the mass. The husband would be compelled insofar as possible to exercise his authority, in Calvin's words, "with modera-tion and not insult over the woman who has been given him [by God] as his partner." Thus, in a real innovation in Christian Europe, men who beat their wives were haled before Consistories and threatened with denial of communion. The men grumbled and complained—"I beat my wife

before and I'll beat her again if she be bad," said a Lyon typecaster—but the situation had improved enough in Geneva by the end of the century that some called it "the women's Paradise."

But despite all this, the Reformed model of the marriage relation subjected the wife to her husband as surely as did the Catholic one. Women had been created sub-ject to men, said Calvin, although before the fall "this was a liberal and gentle sub-jection." Through sin, it had become worse: "Let the woman be satisfied with her state of subjection, and not take it amiss that she is made inferior to the more distinguished sex." Nor was this view re-stricted to pastors. There are many examples from sixteenth-century France of Protestant husbands instructing their wives, "their dear sisters and loyal spouses," telling them of their religious duties, telling them of their responsibilities toward their children, warn-ing them that they must never do anything without seeking advice first. And if Protes-tant wives then told their husbands to go to the devil or otherwise insulted them so loudly that the neighbors heard, the women might soon find themselves brought before the Consistories and even punished (as the criminal records of Geneva reveal) by three days in prison on bread and water.

Undoubtedly there were many Re-formed marriages in commercial and arti-sanal circles where the husbands and wives lived together in peace and friendship. And why not? Women had joined the Reforma-tion to rebel against priests and pope, not to rebel against their husbands. Although they wanted certain "masculine" religious activi-ties opened to them, Calvinist wives—even the most unruly of them—never went so far as to deny the theory of the subjection of women within marriage. The practice of subjection in individual marriages during those heroic decades of the Reformation may have been tempered by two things: first, the personality of the wife herself, which sustained her revolt against priestly power and her search for new relations with books and men; and second, the common cause of reform, which for a while demanded courageous action from both husbands and wives.

And what could a city woman accomplish for the cause if she were not rich and powerful like a noblewoman? On a Catholic feast day, she could defy her Catholic neighbors by sitting ostentatiously spinning in her window. She could puzzle over the Bible alone or with her husband or with Protestant friends. If she were a printer's wife or widow, she could help get out a Protestant edition to spread the word about tyrannical priests. She could use her house for an illegal Protestant conventicle or assembly. She could put aside her dissolute hoop skirts and full gowns and start to wear black. She could harangue priests in the streets. She could march singing songs in defiance of royal edicts. She could smash statues, break baptismal fonts, and destroy holy images. She could, if persecution became very serious, flee to London or Geneva, perhaps the longest trip she had ever taken. She could stay in France and dig the foundations for a Reformed temple. She could even fight—as in Toulouse, where a Huguenot woman bore arms in the First Religious War. And she could die in flames, shouting to her husband, as did one young wife of Langres, "My friend, if we have been joined in marriage in body, think that this is only like a promise of marriage, for our Lord . . . will marry us the day of our martyrdom."

Many of these actions, such as Bible-reading, clearly were special to Protestant city women. A few were not. The Catholic city women in Elizabethan England, for instance, hid priests in their quarters and, if captured, went to the "marriage" of martyrdom as bravely as did any Huguenot. It was the same among the radical Anabaptists. One kind of action, however, seems to have been special to Catholic city women (as also to the radical Quaker women of the seventeenth century): organized group action among women. On the highest level, this was expressed in such attempts to create new forms of common life and work among females as the Ursulines . . . . On the lowest level, this was reflected in the violent activity of all-female Catholic crowds—throwing stones at Protestant women, throwing mire at pastors, and, in the case of a group of female butchers in Aix-en-Provence, beating and hanging the wife of a Protestant bookseller.

These contrasts can point the way to some general conclusions about the long-range significance of the Reformed solution for relations between the sexes. In an interesting essay, Alice Rossi suggests three models for talking about equality. One is assimilationist: the subordinate group is somewhat raised by making it like the superior group. A second is pluralistic: each group is allowed to keep its distinctive characteristics but within a context of society at large that is still hierarchical. The third is hybrid (or, better, transformational), involving changes within and among all groups involved. Whatever transformations in social relations were accomplished by either the Reformation or the Counter-Reformation, it seems that as far as relations between the sexes go the Reformed solution was assimilationist; the Catholic solution, with its female saints and convents, was pluralistic. Neither, of course, eliminated the subject status of women.

Is one position clearly better than the other? That is, within the context of the society of the sixteenth and seventeenth centuries did one solution seem to offer greater freedom to men and women to make decisions about their lives and to adopt new roles? One important school of sociologists always answers such questions in favor of Protestantism. It is the superior sect: its transcendent and activist Father, less hierarchical religious symbolism, and this-worldly asceticism all make for a more evolved religion, facilitating the desacralization of society. More different choices are also facilitated, so this argument goes, and more rapid social change.

Certainly it is true that the Reformed solution did promote a certain desexualization of society, a certain neutralizing of forms of communication and of certain religious places so that they became acceptable for women. These were important gains, bringing new tools to women and new experience to both sexes. But the assimilationist solution brought losses, too. This worldly asceticism denied laymen and laywomen much of the shared recreational and festive life allowed them by Catholicism. It closed off an institutionalized and respectable alternative to private family life: the communal living of the monastery. By destroying the female saints as exemplars for both sexes, it cut off a wide range of affect and activity. And by eliminating a separate identity and separate organization for women in religious life, it may have made them a little more vulnerable to subjection in all spheres.

As it turned out, women suffered for their powerlessness in both Catholic and Protestant lands in the late sixteenth to eighteenth centuries as changes in marriage laws restricted the freedoms of wives even further, as female guilds dwindled, as the female role in middle-level commerce and farm direction contracted, and as the differential between male and female wages increased. In both Catholic France and Protestant England, the learned lady struggled to establish a role for herself: the female schoolteacher became a familiar figure, whether as a spinster or as an Ursuline; the female dramatist scrambled to make a living . . . .

Thus it is hard to establish from a historical point of view that the Reformed assimilationist structure always facilitated more rapid and creative changes in sex roles than did the relatively pluralistic structure found in the Catholicism of the sixteenth and seventeenth centuries. Both forms of religious life have contributed to the transformation of sex roles and to the transformation of society. In the proper circumstances, each can serve as a corrective to the other.

States General
of the United Netherlands

DECLARATION OF INDEPENDENCE
BY THE UNITED NETHERLANDS

This striking document reflects the interaction of political, economic, and religious factors involved in a nation's struggle for independence. In this instance, champions of religious change successfully combined their efforts with those seeking political self-determination. Students of history will note that this statement has remarkable similarities to a much better known declaration of independence issued almost two centuries later.

From E. H. Kossman and A. F. Mellink, eds., *Texts Concerning the Revolt of the Netherlands* (Cambridge University Press, Cambridge, 1974), pp. 216-221, 225-226. Reprinted by permission of the Cambridge University Press.

THE STATES General of the United Netherlands greet all those who will see or hear this read.

It is common knowledge that the prince of a country is appointed by God to be the head of his subjects to protect and shield them from all iniquity, trouble and violence as a shepherd is called to protect his sheep, and that the subjects are not created by God for the benefit of the prince, to submit to all that he decrees, whether godly or ungodly, just or unjust, and to serve him as slaves. On the contrary, the prince is created for the subjects (without whom he cannot be a prince) to govern them according to right and reason and defend and love them as a father does his children and a shepherd does his sheep when he risks his body and life for their safety. It is clear therefore that if he acts differently and instead of protecting his subjects endeavours to oppress and molest them and to deprive them of their ancient liberty, privileges and customs and to command and use them like slaves, he must be regarded not as a prince but as a tyrant. And according to right and reason his subjects, at any rate, must no longer recognise him as a prince (notably when this is decided by the States of the country), but should renounce him; in his stead another must be elected to be an overlord called to protect them. This becomes even more true when these subjects have been unable either to soften their prince's heart through explanations humbly made or to turn him away from his tyrannical enterprises, and have no other means left to protect their ancient liberty (for the defence of which they must according to the law of nature be prepared to risk life and property) as well as that of their wives, children and descendants. This has often happened for similar reasons in many other countries at various times and there are well known instances of it. And this should happen particularly in these countries, which have always been governed (as they should be) in accordance with the oath taken by the prince at his inauguration and in conformity with the privileges, customs and old traditions of these countries which he swears to maintain. Moreover, nearly all these coun-

tries have accepted their prince conditionally, by contracts and agreements and if the prince breaks them, he legally forfeits his sovereignty.

After the death of the emperor Charles V who is remembered with respect and who left all these Netherlands to him the king of Spain forgot the services which these countries and subjects had rendered his father and himself and which made it possible for him to achieve such glorious victories over his enemies that his fame and power came to be talked of and respected throughout the world; similarly he forgot the admonitions made by His Imperial Majesty in the past and lent his ear to and put his trust in members of the Council of Spain which was at his side. These persons, most of whom knew of the wealth and the power of these countries, envied them and their liberty, because they could not be made governors of them or acquire high office in them as they could in the kingdoms of Naples and Sicily, in Milan and the Indies and other places within the king's realm. This Council of Spain or some of its most prominent members repeatedly remonstrated with the king, asserting that it would be better for his reputation and majesty if he conquered these territories again so that he might rule them freely and absolutely (that is, tyrannise over them at his will) instead of governing them according to the conditions and under such restrictions as he had been bound on oath to agree when he took over the sovereignty of these countries.

Ever since, on their advice the king has been trying to deprive these countries of their ancient freedom and to bring them into slavery under Spanish rule. First he intended to appoint new bishops to the most important and powerful towns under the pretext of protecting religion. He endowed these magnificently by appending to their sees the richest abbeys and attaching to each of them nine canons as councillors, three with special responsibility for the inquisition. Through the incorporation of the abbeys the bishops, who might equally well be foreigners as natives, would have acquired the foremost places and votes in the assemblies of the States of these countries, and would have been the king's creatures, totally submissive and devoted to him. Through the appointment of the canons the king would have introduced the Spanish inquisition in these countries where (as is generally known) it has always been held to be as abominable and odious as the worst slavery. When once His Imperial Majesty proposed to establish it in these countries, his subjects submitted a remonstrance which made him withdraw the project. Thus he displayed the sincere affection he felt for them.

Various written remonstrances were submitted to the king by towns and provinces and verbal complaints were made by two prominent nobles of the country, the lord of Montigny and the count of Egmont. With the consent of the duchess of Parma, then regent of these countries, and on the advice of the Council of State and the States General, these nobles were in turn sent to Spain. Although the king of Spain gave them verbal assurances that he would comply with their request, shortly afterwards he sent written orders that the bishops should be received immediately, on penalty of incurring his wrath, and put in possession of their bishoprics and incorporated abbeys, and that the inquisition be enforced where it had existed before and the decrees of the Council of Trent be executed (this was in various ways contrary to the privileges of the said countries). When all this became generally known, it naturally gave rise to much alarm among the people and the great affection which as faithful subjects they had always felt for the king of Spain and his forebears greatly diminished. They were particularly shocked by these events because they noticed that the king was not only trying to tyrannize over their persons and possessions but also over their consciences. For these they thought to have to answer to none but God alone.

Thus, in 1566, out of pity for the people the most prominent members of this country's nobility submitted a remonstrance to his Majesty. In this they asked him to mitigate his policy relating to the strict inquisition and punishment in matters of religion, in order to appease the people and to prevent all sedition, and moreover to show thereby the love and affection which as a merciful prince he felt for his subjects. At the request of the regent, of the Council of State and of the States General of all these countries, the marquess of Bergen and the lord of Montigny were sent to Spain as ambassadors to explain all these matters further and to speak with greater authority to the king of Spain. They were to make it clear how necessary it was for the prosperity and tranquillity of the country to abandon such innovations and to mitigate the rigorous penalties for infringing the religious edicts. But instead of listening to these envoys and providing against the ill consequences about which he was warned (these had already started to manifest themselves among the people in most provinces since the necessary remedies had been delayed so long) the king surrendered to the pressures of the Spanish Council and declared that the people who had submitted this remonstrance were rebels and guilty of the crime of *laesae majestatis* and as such liable to punishment by death and confiscation. Moreover (because he firmly believed that the duke of Alva's violent measures had totally subjected the provinces to his power and tyranny) he acted against all fundamental rights, always strictly maintained by even the most cruel and tyrannical princes, and committed the said noble envoys to prison, had them put to death and had their possessions confiscated.

And although the disturbances caused in the year 1566 by the actions of the regent and her adherents had been virtually quelled and many of those who defended the liberty of the country had been driven out and the others subjugated so that the king no longer had the remotest reason for suppressing these countries with force of arms, he nevertheless—showing, contrary to his duty as their prince, protector and good shepherd, his lack of affection towards his loyal subjects—gave in to the advice of the Spanish Council. It is clear from the letters—which were intercepted—of Alana, the Spanish ambassador in France, to the duchess of

Parma, written in those days, that the council had for a long time been seeking and hoping for an opportunity to abolish all the privileges of the country and to have it tyrannically governed by Spaniards like the Indies and newly conquered countries. Thus the king sent the duke of Alva and a large army to these provinces to suppress their liberties. The duke was notorious for his severity and cruelty, he was one of the principal enemies of these countries and was accompanied by advisers of the same nature and mentality.

The duke of Alva entered these countries without meeting any resistance and was received by their poor inhabitants with great respect and honour. They expected only mercy and clemency, for in his letters the king had often hypocritically promised them this. He had even written that he intended to come personally to these countries to arrange everything to everybody's satisfaction. At the time of the duke of Alva's departure the king had a fleet of ships equipped in Spain to carry him and another in Zeeland to meet him—which put the country to great expense—in order to deceive and ensnare his subjects. In spite of this the duke of Alva who was a foreigner and not related to the king, declared immediately upon his arrival that the king had appointed him commander-in-chief, and shortly afterwards even governor-general of the country. This was contrary to the privileges and ancient traditions. And making his intentions quite clear he immediately put troops into the principal towns and fortresses and built castles and fortifications in the most important and powerful towns to keep them subdued. On behalf of the king and in kindly terms he bade the highest nobles come to him under the pretext of needing their advice and of wishing to employ them in the service of the country. But those who complied with his invitation were imprisoned and contrary to the privileges removed from Brabant where they had been seized. He had them tried before him, although he was not competent to be their judge, and then, without completing their trial, sentenced them to death and had them publicly and ignominiously

executed. Others, more aware of the hypocrisy of the Spaniards, left the country but were for this condemned by Alva to forfeit their life and possessions. Thus the poor inhabitants, having lost their fortresses and the princes who could defend their freedom, would be helpless in the face of Spanish violence.

Moreover he put to death or drove away innumerable other nobles and excellent citizens so as to be able to confiscate their goods; he lodged common Spanish soldiers in the houses of the other inhabitants and these molested them, their wives and children and damaged their property; and he levied many and manifold taxes. He forced the people to contribute to the building of new castles and fortifications in the towns—erected for their own oppression; he forced them to pay the hundredth, twentieth and tenth penny for the support of the soldiers whom he brought with him and those whom he recruited here and who were to be used against their fellow-countrymen and against those who risked their lives to defend the liberty of the country. Thus the people would become so poor that they would not be able to prevent him from fully carrying out his plan to execute the orders he had received in Spain—to treat the country as though it were newly conquered . . . .

Nevertheless we have not ceased to attempt through humble letters and through the mediation of the most important princes of Christendom to reconcile ourselves and to make peace with the king. Indeed, until quite recently we kept envoys in Cologne, hoping that through the mediation of His Imperial Majesty and the Electors who took part in the negotiations we might obtain a firm peace guaranteeing some freedom granted in mercy, principally freedom of religion for this mainly concerns God and men's consciences. But from experience we learned that we could obtain nothing from the king by such remonstrances and meetings, for the only purpose of these negotiations was to sow discord among the provinces and to divide them. Thereafter the king hoped that he would be able to subdue them more easily one after another and to realise with the utmost severity what he had from the outset intended against them. This was afterwards clearly shown by an edict of proscription which the king published in order to render the inhabitants of the provinces universally hated, to impede their trade and to bring them into utter despair. For he declared that we and all the officials and inhabitants of the united provinces and their adherents were rebels and as such had forfeited our lives and estates; furthermore he set a large sum of money on the head of the prince of Orange.

Therefore, despairing of all means of reconciliation and left without any other remedies and help, we have been forced (in conformity with the law of nature and for the protection of our own rights and those of our fellow-countrymen, of the privileges, traditional customs and liberties of the fatherland, the life and honour of our wives, children and descendants so that they should not fall into Spanish slavery) to abandon the king of Spain and to pursue such means as we think likely to secure our rights, privileges and liberties.

Therefore we make it known that for all these reasons, forced by utter necessity, we have declared and declare herewith by a common accord, decision and agreement that the king of Spain has *ipso jure* forfeited his lordship, jurisdiction and inheritance of these provinces, that we do not intend to recognise him in any matters concerning him personally, his sovereignty, jurisdiction and domains in these countries, nor to use or to permit others to use his name as that of our sovereign. Consequently we declare all officers, judges, lords with lower jurisdiction, vassals and all other inhabitants of these provinces, whatever their condition or quality, to be henceforward released from all obligations and oaths they may have sworn to the king of Spain as lord of these countries.

CONCLUSION

FOR CENTURIES economic grievances, anticlericalism, social unrest,
political tension, and other factors
had fed the stream of popular discontent.
Early in the sixteenth century it became a
raging torrent that threatened to sweep away
everything in its path. No one could possibly
know that Luther's protest would provide
the occasion for bringing together widely
divergent streams of societal discontent.

When the Diet of Worms issued its sharp
attack on ecclesiastical practices, the casual
observer might have concluded that Luther
and the Diet were in agreement. Both
seemed to focus their attack on the religious
establishment. Basic differences, however,
became clearly apparent when Luther was
condemned by the Edict of Worms. But
what, precisely, was the difference in the
positions taken by the Diet and by Luther?
The selections from the statement issued by
the Diet and from Luther's later reminis-
cences suggest some of these differences.
Subsequent events demonstrated that the
differences were basic and crucial, for the
goals of Luther, as depicted by Ritter, were
theological rather than social, economic, or
political. At the same time, Luther's actions
did generate a great deal of revolutionary
"fallout," for opponents of the old political
and ecclesiastical systems welcomed aid
from any source.

The excerpt from Steinmetz indicates
just how difficult reform in any one area
might be, especially in a society where
modern conceptions of separation of church
and state were as foreign as Martians. The
twentieth-century mind may sometimes find
it difficult to envision a world so different
from our own. At first glance, attempts to
reshape the "early bourgeois" society may
appear strange because of their religious
trappings, yet an examination of the forces
of discontent demonstrates the broad spectrum of people who were determined to
reform their community. Frequently, proponents of change were united in their
definition of the enemy, even though desired
changes varied greatly.

Goals of participants in the Reformation differed substantially, and it is hardly
surprising that methods used were also frequently at variance with each other. One of
the old assumptions about determining a
community's stance toward the Reformation
was well expressed by a historian of the past
century who wrote, *"Alles kommt von
Oben"* ("Everything comes from above").
But was the role of princes and other
officials necessarily the decisive factor in
defining goals and determining methods? In
a society where power was exercised by the
few—often the very few—did the citizenry
really figure significantly in the decision-
making process?

Certainly many aspects of society were
in a state of flux, and the masses constituted
part of this uncertainty. Yet, goaded on by a
skillful leader, the discontented populace
often proved fertile ground for dramatic,
and sometimes decisive, change. By sheer
force of numbers and strategic location a
crowd on a city square might well overawe a
hesitant city council. But did such an
aroused populace sometimes mistake the
form of power for its substance? The selections from Elton, Hillerbrand and Hall provide provocative comments on the dynamics
of change in a turbulent age. Certainly
crowds could be manipulated, and this fact
often made the masses potentially powerful,
but also often unpredictable.

One of the areas in which the Reformation effected change is in forms of cultural
expression. Some historians have suggested
that the arts fared badly wherever the
Reformation triumphed; others have suggested that the Reformation accelerated
cultural change and modified societal attitudes. Did the Reformation bring greater
opportunity and equality for women? Professor Davis has provided some keen insights
into the changing role of women, while the
essay by Imogen Luxton suggests that the
power of the pen proved a significant factor
in effecting cultural change.

By the end of the sixteenth century,
documents such as the Declaration of Inde-

pendence issued by the rebelling estates in the Netherlands, moved religion off center stage and assigned it a less conspicuous role. Appeals to natural law and insistence on the rights of people suggested that powerful forces of secularization were reshaping society. As the century of the Reformation drew to a close, the distinctive elements of the Reformation were being supplanted by new forces.

SUGGESTIONS FOR ADDITIONAL READING

THE LITERATURE on the Reformation is massive. Serious scholars will find a wealth of information in bibliographies such as Karl Schottenloher, *Bibliographie zur deutschen Geschichte im Zeitalter der Glaubensspaltung* (Leipzig and Stuttgart, 1933-1962); Roland Bainton, *Bibliography of the Continental Reformation* (Chicago, 1935); and in Roland Bainton and Eric Gritsch, *Bibliography of the Continental Reformation: Materials Available in English* (Hamden, Conn., 1972).

Among the general histories of the Reformation, the following have appeared recently: G.R. Elton, *Reformation Europe, 1517-1559* (New York, 1963); Harold J. Grimm, *The Reformation Era, 1500-1650* (New York, 1965); Hans J. Hillerbrand, *Christendom Divided: The Protestant Reformation* (New York, 1971); Lewis W. Spitz, *The Renaissance and the Reformation Movements* (Chicago, 1971); Peter J. Klassen, *Europe in the Reformation* (Englewood Cliffs, 1979).

Captivating contemporary documents have been used to present a graphic account of the Reformation movement in the following works: Hans J. Hillerbrand, ed., *The Reformation: A Narrative History Related by Contemporary Observers and Participants* (New York, 1964) and Oskar Thulin, ed., *Illustrated History of the Reformation* (St. Louis, 1967).

English translations of many treatises of major reformers, as well as chroniclers' reports and political statements, will be found in the following books of readings: Roland Bainton, ed., *The Age of the Reformation* (New York, 1956); John Dillenberger, ed., *Martin Luther: Selections* (Garden City, N. Y., 1961); Lewis W. Spitz, ed., *The Protestant Reformation* (Englewood Cliffs, 1966); Hans J. Hillerbrand, ed., *The Protestant Reformation* (New York, 1968).

Numerous biographies of prominent figures in the Reformation have appeared, although no other leader of that age approaches Luther in the literature devoted to him. Among the accounts of Luther's life, none has captured the imagination of readers so thoroughly as has Roland Bainton, *Here I Stand: A Life of Martin Luther* (New York, 1950). Studies by Heinrich Boehmer, *Road to Reformation* (Philadelphia, 1946); Gordon Rupp, *Luther's Progress to the Diet of Worms* (London, 1951); and A. G. Dickens, *Luther and the Reformation* (London, 1967), examine the reformer in relation to contemporary social, religious, and political problems. Erik Erikson, in his *Young Man Luther* (New York, 1958), touched off a vigorous controversy when he presented his psychoanalytical study of the reformer.

In recent years, economic and social factors have received increasing attention from numerous scholars. Many of the Marxist studies have not yet appeared in English translation. Valuable insights are developed in M. M. Smirin, *Die Volksreformation des Thomas Müntzer und der grosse Bauernkrieg* (Berlin, 1952); Gerhard Zschäbitz, *Martin Luther: Grösse und Grenze* (Berlin, 1967); and Max Steinmetz, *Der deutsche Bauernkrieg und Thomas Müntzer* (Leipzig, 1976). A thorough evaluation of the Marxist approach to the Reformation is given in Abraham Friesen, *Reformation and Utopia: The Marxist Interpretation of the Reformation and Its Antecedents* (Wiesbaden, 1974). The central figure in the Peasants' War is given scholarly analysis in Eric W. Gritsch, *Reformer Without a Church* (Philadelphia, 1967).

Important interpretations of forces that shaped the Reformation community are examined in G. E. Swanson, *Religion and Regime* (Ann Arbor, 1967); Kyle Session, ed., *Reformation and Authority: The Meaning of the Peasants' Revolt* (Lexington, 1968); Steven Ozment, *The Reformation in the Cities* (New Haven, 1975); and in Miriam C. Chrisman and Otto Gründler, ed., *Social Groups and Religious Ideas in the Sixteenth Century* (Kalamazoo, 1978).

For a lively discussion of life in the Reformation city, the following books are especially stimulating: Gerald Strauss, *Nuremberg in the Sixteenth Century* (New York, 1966) and Miriam Chrisman, *Strasbourg and the Reform* (New Haven, 1967).

An avalanche of pamphlet literature, as well as broadsides and cartoons, depicted the robust spirit of the age. Discussions of these phenomena are presented in Arnold Berger, *Die Sturmtruppen der Reformation: Ausgewählte Flugschriften der Jahre 1520-1525* (Leipzig, 1931); O. Clemen, ed., *Flugschriften aus den ersten Jahren der Reformation* (Nieuwkoop, 1967); and in John Bohnstedt, *The Infidel Scourge of God* (Philadelphia, 1968).

Women in the Reformation are receiving increased attention. Fascinating vignettes are presented in Roland Bainton's trilogy: *Women of the Reformation in Germany and Italy* (Minneapolis, 1971); *Women of the Reformation in France and England* (Minneapolis, 1973); *Women of the Reformation, from Spain to Scandinavia* (Minneapolis, 1977). More detailed analyses will be found in studies such as Nancy Roelker, *Queen of Navarre: Jeanne d'Albret, 1528-1572*

(Cambridge, Mass., 1972) and Natalie Z. Davis, *Society and Culture in Early Modern France* (Stanford, 1975).

The Reformation has long been viewed as having been important in shaping political thought. Church-state relations are surveyed in Peter J. Klassen, *Church and State in Reformation Europe* (St. Louis, 1975). Calvinism's impact upon political systems is examined in G. L. Hunt, ed., *Calvinism and the Political Order* (Philadelphia, 1965), while the reformer's ideas are analyzed in François Wendel, *Calvin: The Origins and Development of His Political Thought*, trans. by P. Mairet (New York, 1963). Interpretive surveys are presented in H. G. Koenigsberger, *Estates and Revolutions* (Ithaca, 1971). Since Calvinism was the strongest Protestant movement involved in the religious wars in France and the Netherlands, it plays a prominent role in these accounts of those turbulent years: Pieter Geyl, *The Revolt of the Netherlands* (New York, 1958); J. H. M. Salmon, ed., *The French Wars of Religion: How Important Were Religious Factors?* (Boston, 1967); and in Robert M. Kingdon, *Geneva and the Consolidation of the French Protestant Movement, 1564-1572* (Madison, 1967).